T0098404

RAJA RAO

# *The Sacred Wordsmith*

## WRITING AND THE WORD

PENGUIN BOOKS

An imprint of Penguin Random House

PENGUIN BOOKS

USA | Canada | UK | Ireland | Australia
New Zealand | India | South Africa | China

Penguin Books is part of the Penguin Random House group of companies
whose addresses can be found at global.penguinrandomhouse.com

Published by Penguin Random House India Pvt. Ltd
4th Floor, Capital Tower 1, MG Road,
Gurugram 122 002, Haryana, India

First published in India in Penguin Books by Penguin Random House India 2022

Text and Introduction copyright © Susan Raja-Rao—The Legal Heir(s) of Raja Rao 2022

All rights reserved

10 9 8 7 6 5 4 3 2 1

The views and opinions expressed in this book are the author's own and the
facts are as reported by him which have been verified to the extent possible,
and the publishers are not in any way liable for the same.

ISBN 9780143448624

Typeset in Bembo Std by Manipal Technologies Limited, Manipal

This book is sold subject to the condition that it shall not, by way of trade
or otherwise, be lent, resold, hired out, or otherwise circulated without the
publisher's prior consent in any form of binding or cover other than that in
which it is published and without a similar condition including this condition
being imposed on the subsequent purchaser.

www.penguin.co.in

PENGUIN MODERN CLASSICS
*The Sacred Wordsmith*

RAJA RAO, a path-breaker of Indian writing in English, was born in Hassan, Mysore. He has been awarded the Padma Vibhushan, the Sahitya Akademi Award and the Neustadt International Prize for Literature.

Therefore, the purification of the word is (the means to the) attainment of the Supreme Self. One who knows the essence of its activity attains the immortal Brahman.

Bhartrihari Vakyapada.1.131

# Contents

## Part II
### Vac, the Word

## Part III
### The Interviews

# Preface

All the universe is ultimately nothing but meaning, the Word, pure knowledge. You yourself are pure knowledge undifferentiated, though you think you are differentiated—and from there comes the trouble, the misunderstanding of the Word. When differentiating yourself from the world, you do so as well from the meaning of the Word.

The true literary creator, or reader, is he who lives in undifferentiated silence, and worships this silence in such a way that the silence worships itself in vibratory sound. For the serious writer, this is a spiritual experience, leading him or her to the Absolute.

In the dissolution of the Word there is joy. In the dissolution of the ego, the Absolute. In that sense, all words, all literature are prayers to take you from your ego-ridden condition to the Absolute, the Truth.

Raja Rao, 1967
Excerpt from his speech
'Quest for the Word'

# Introduction

## Raja Rao at His Bed Table

Raja Rao, the Sacred Wordsmith, is no longer.

His small grey typewriter sits idle in the closet, leaning against boxes full of the manuscripts he brought to life with its keys. He always wrote in bed. Propped up by pillows, he would sit upright—his rectangular eight-inch tall dark brown handcrafted writing table before him. Over the years, he'd tapped out thousands of precious pages on his ancient Hermes-Rocket manual typewriter. Occasionally, he broke into longhand, often so illegibly that even he could hardly decipher what he had scribbled down.

From a young age, Raja knew he would be a writer. Born to a Brahmin family—Vedantin priests and advisors to kings since the thirteenth century—he grew up with a profound knowledge of classical Indian philosophy and culture. Even as a boy, he was convinced writing was his dharma, what one is born to do. The act of writing was his *sadhana*, the practice taken up to reach one's spiritual goal. His metaphysical and literary quests were interwoven. He was committed to fulfilling his dharma no matter what the consequences—be they poverty, starvation, even death.

He never wrote for money, fame, or an audience—only for the sake of his dharma. In his early years, he wanted to publish anonymously, but his publisher would not allow it. Raja often said that when one follows his dharma, with no thought of reward, the universe itself comes to help, opening all doors. He lived his dharma more devotedly than any human being I've ever known, following his path with absolute commitment, unshakeable courage, and unbounded joyous enthusiasm.

Raja so reverenced the word, he never used abbreviations or colloquialisms; he abhorred American slang. In the twenty-six years we were together, I not once heard him utter a frivolous word. He disliked creative-writing classes; indeed, was adamantly opposed to all mental manipulations of the word. He understood that the true art of writing arises, beyond the personal self, from one's inmost being. He always said, 'The word is sacred, and writing is worship.' When awarded the 1988 Neustadt Prize for Literature, in his acceptance speech, he stated, 'I am a man of silence. And words emerge from that silence with light. And light is sacred . . . The writer or poet is he who seeks back the common word to its origin of silence, that the manifested word become light.'

He would initiate his work sessions in two ways—the first and most dramatic when seized by a burning desire to write. This might come upon him at any time. Many a night I would be awakened by noise, bright lights, and Raja racing wildly around our room shouting, 'Where is my paper? I need my paper and pen!' After helping him find these, I would arrange his pillows on the bed, situate his writing table, then either leave the room or he would ask me to stay and lie silently beside him. He would work for one or two hours, perhaps begin a new novel or essay, or continue one in progress. What arose was unimagined by him until that moment, unplanned and unknown. It burst forth as pure expression, from the very depths of his being.

The other form his writing sessions took was methodical and planned, his early mornings spent in grave preparation for this. Upon awakening, he would meditate, eat breakfast, then spend a peaceful hour walking a nearby nature trail. This was followed by a shower and another brief meditation. His final preparation was a purifying ritual, sprinkling sanctified water on himself, bed table, typewriter, and writing area, all the while intoning a mantra. Whether he was working on a novel, essay, or a speech for a conference, these sessions, though orderly, were born of the same inspired state of consciousness revealed in his explosive outpourings. Both approaches to his writing bore the same level of exalted beauty. He wrote in absolute solitude, for several hours, silent, inwardly absorbed, as at night. While a disciplined Raja worked day after day on a project, once finished, he might write nothing for long periods of time. Suddenly motivated by some mysterious spark of creativity, he would resume his daily routine.

At the age of thirty, however, his life would be upended. After having achieved much fame and success, he realized he could go no further, vowing never to write again until he found his ultimate spiritual goal, his Sat Guru. For several years he searched for Him, seeking out and listening to such revered Indian teachers as Pandit Taranath, Sri Aurobindo, Sri Krishnamurti, Mahatma Gandhi, and Ramana Maharshi.

Though deeply moved by these great men, he knew none was *his* Guru. While staying in Maharshi's ashram, Raja reached a point of utter despair, thinking he would never find his true Guru. Unexpectedly, an Englishman living at the Ashram told him where he could find what he was searching for. In later years, he loved to recount the story of how an *Englishman,* of all people, led him by the hand to his Sat Guru, Sri Atmananda of Trivandrum. 'And Sri Atmananda answered all my questions of one hundred lives,' Raja would say.

But as an initiate in the Guru's home, Raja had yet to take up his writing. One day, Sri Atmananda asked him, 'Raja, what are you doing?' To which he replied, 'Nothing at all.' The Guru then instructed, 'I think you should begin writing again.' He took up his pen with the philosophical essay 'The Song of Love', followed eventually by his internationally acclaimed novel, *The Serpent and the Rope.* He went on to write several more novels, short stories, fables, and an assortment of non-fiction books—essays, articles, and speeches numbering in the hundreds. Many of these works remain unpublished. The pinnacle of his literary pilgrimage is the trilogy *The Chessmaster and His Moves*—its two thousand pages typed on that same little typewriter, while sitting in bed. Only the first volume has been published, the other two are currently being edited. The Sacred Wordsmith Raja Rao Memorial Endowment was created in 2009, with the mission to make his entire archive available to the world.

After meeting Sri Atmananda, Raja's creative genius turned solely inward. As he grew spiritually, his writing continued to evolve, reaching ever more transcendent heights throughout his long life, and with genuine humility, he would confess,

'What is good about my writing belongs to The Guru. The mistakes are mine.'

\* \* \*

'The language we write must equate our being,' states Raja Rao in his essay 'The Word'. He didn't merely write about the Vedantic principles illustrated in the present book; he lived them. In another essay, 'Dissolution is Fulfillment,' he quotes from the great Bhartrihari's *Vakyapadia*: 'Linguistics, or *vyakarana* is the road to salvation.' In his pursuit of writing as a spiritual path, Raja was the personification of this quote.

Late afternoon or early evening was a favourite time for us. Raja, then, would read aloud what he'd written during the day. He often asked me if a certain word, line, or phrase needed correction, but to me these were always perfect. If he did make corrections, it was usually to polish words—until what seemed impossible to improve was rendered even more exquisite.

He would read from bed while I sat in a chair facing him. We knew the writing was true when its breathtaking beauty transported both of us into a deep silence—where we remained, unmoving, as the evening fell.

\* \* \*

The book before you, indeed all of Raja Rao's works, reflect the story of his life, a deeply Indian story. I was always aware he, though born into a modern age, was an embodiment of ancient Indian wisdom and culture. As I grew to understand the traditional south–Asian arc of his life, I came to discover he was the epitome of a true Brahmin, a keeper of India's spiritual legacy. In characterizing the magnificent Rabindranath Tagore in his essay, 'Tagore: Renascence Man', Raja could be describing himself when he said, 'He might have been a host in the middle of a peaceful and luxuriant forest, the master teaching his pupils in the time of the Upanishads.'

People often questioned Raja's devotion to India because he lived much of his life abroad. Though destiny dictated he reside in Europe and America, in truth he never left India, carrying his beloved homeland with him wherever he travelled. He was never changed by other cultures, instead changing them through the power of his presence. Author, professor, philosopher, orator, he occupies a hallowed place in the pantheon of great men and women, he whose dharma was to help bring Indian wisdom to the West.

Beyond all this, beyond everything, he was a devoted disciple of his Sat Guru, Sri Atmananda.

The Sacred Wordsmith Raja Rao Memorial Endowment, the steward of his legacy, is privileged to present this collection, the first offering from his unpublished archive.

# The World Is Sound

The world is *sabda*, sound.

When the Vedas sound not primary sound, there's chaos. Crack and commotion and clash occur, as if the titans were at war with the gods. The grass grows stump, the stars grow dim, man is dwarfed by his penis. Man's disproportions, though, are as nothing when the earth and the sky and the merry-go-round of stars jumble in such discord—when hot air and cold fight as two serpents, the mountains burn, the dogs strike, the lions yawn, the atoms misorientate. The cleavage in the ether creates concussions between the planetary ellipses.

Sound hoards harmony as meaning. With sound disturbed, it is as if the notes are freed from temperament, catapulting their ways to lonely paths, dishevelled. The melodic *raginis,* whose birth and death are the intake and outgoing of breath, wail as white, cold valley winds. But their lamentations go unheard. Nothing happens. The gods are lost. Will the Titans prevail?

Epoch-deep is Brahma's sleep. When the circle meets the point or the light—plasma touches its own tail—there's such a clashing silence that Vishnu is awakened. What's this happening? He wonders. The serpent under Him holds its breath for fear that the Lord might awaken too quickly and all would be burnt to ash. The waters at His feet spin on themselves, leaping and dissolving, fearful of conflagration. Arising at His side, Lakshmi weeps, tears falling from Her eyes onto the lotus stalk beneath. The hairs on Vishnu's body lift. His eyelashes breathe, His skin suddenly blue. He hears *sa* against *ri* and *ma* against *pa*, and yet the raginis come not. Still not opening His eyes, He calls for Indra-Ragini!

There's no answer, no sound. When He does open His eyes, He sees sound like little worms eating each other, long and short, big and small, red and white, chomping one another as they would chutney. Blood is good, flesh is musty, licking your tongue is sexual delight. You live and die; the Titans are faring well.

Vishnu again calls for the raginis. And again there's no sound but for a funeral drumbeat, taka-dhimi, taka-dhimi. Silence hits against itself, until Vishnu's voice reaches His thyroarytenoid vortex—only then is there sound. Wild with rage, He again shouts, 'Indra-Ragini!' The universe trembles. Such is the fear, the chaos, that Shiva rushes from the Himalayas seeking Lord Vishnu's guidance.

'What is happening?' asks Vishnu of the Trident-bearer.

'Great Lord Creator-Preserver,' cries Shiva, 'the world is knit with night. Sagara, the great King of the blessed Isle of the Rose-Apple Tree, having conquered most of the known world, is bent on total domination. Already Lord of many lands, he wants to be the bearer of the supreme umbrella, an emperor endowed with the four signs of sovereignty. He with his sixty thousand sons would perform an *Ashwamedha yagna*, sending the sacrificial horse of victory on its conquering journey.'

'Great was the rejoicement,' Shiva told Vishnu, 'in King Sagara's capital. The Brahmins prayed, the merchants hung gold filigree on their shop doors, and the peasants tilled the earth that the crops be eighty-eight fingers high. The world seemed ripe for possessing.'

'Thus,' Shiva continued, 'with fife and drum did the sacrificial horse set out on its journey. The horse was a bay that had all the thirty-six marks of sacred congruity and a pedigree that could be traced to Indra's own horse, Uchchaihshravas. From Uchchaihshravas was Hitaketu born, and from Hitaketu, Vaishravara, and so on—until now Sagara's bay, adorned with garland, coconut, and holy kumkum mark, vowed unfailing fealty to his King.

'The horse's unguidedly guided steps took him all the way to the very trap door of the earth. Into the netherworld he stepped, travelling it as long as it was long and as broad as it was broad. Whereupon all the creatures of this netherworld also accepted Sagara as the overlord of creation. Atop one of its hills, the famous ascetic Kapila, son of Kardama, sat in meditation, immense in his austerities—this making him burn as pure as the flame of knowledge. The horse, approaching him, innocently stuck its snout above the anchorite's head, and all the sixty thousand sons of Sagara were unable to stop it from nibbling the great Kapila's hair.

'The very fire of all fires then rose out of the ascetic's cranium—the flame that could burn universes, universes of universes, and every finite term of space—and the sixty thousand children of Sagara, with the horse itself, were burnt into ash. Silence fell upon creation; in shock, nobody knew what was what, which was which. And where had the horse gone? Where?'

'Sagara's messengers,' the distraught Shiva went on, 'searched hither and thither over the barren earth. Even the sound of sixty thousand men marching had left no echo in the hills, but their footprints remained. The King's men followed these into the kingdom of the netherworld, and there discovered the sixty thousand sons of Sagara molded into beautiful blue ash. The horse, too. Despite having been dead for many turns of moon and sun, all lay as if the smoke had gone out a wink-moment ago.'

Unable to bear this loss, Sagara, after crowning his son Ansumath in his place, left his kingdom to wander in search of his ultimate askesis. But how, wondered Ansumath, was he to remove the curse of Kapila? Was it even possible? Rising in meditation from level to level, he travelled within himself to find the answer. But none came. Even the gods were mute; answers do not come easily when a sage as powerful as Kapila has cursed a man for an improper act. And with him the world.

The accursed Sagara would die still unenlightened. Sadly, having taken up his father's task, Ansumath, too, would fail. It was then hoped that Dilipa, *his* son, would exorcise the evil that had befallen his great lineage. Dilipa also went from level to level within, beyond even the beyond of concentrated thought.

But still no answer came. The earth grew parched, cattle cried in misery. The very monkeys had no strength to leap from tree to earth, or earth to tree. The elephants, powerless to move, stood frozen as mountain stone. Birds were dead quiet, the lions' manes ragged as coconut rind. The waters of the oceans were drying up. Life had no juice anymore—men no power or breath, stone no shape, rivers no movement. When Dilipa, too, died, his son Bhagiratha vowed, 'I also will go forth, nor shall I cease till the earth is purified. Lord Shiva,' he cried, 'Lord of the Trident, help me!'

'Only then did I, Shiva, shaken from my meditations, awaken, and with high, folded hands prayed to you, O Vishnu, Lord of the Lotus-navel, what am I to do? I, Shiva, dancer of destruction, am neither creator nor preserver. But through my prayer, and the chaos, you slept.'

'Then, in my compassion for Bhagiratha, I fell back into meditation, till even the earth's nexus shook, and Adi Sesha—the foremost of snakes who floats in the ocean of the changing world and forms the bed of Vishnu—woke from his torpor. Now, however, that you, Lord Vishnu, have risen from *your* sleep, shower on us your benevolence. Give back man his breath, his virility, his water.'

Vishnu now understood. For He saw at His feet the waters leaping, revolving, going round and round in a circle like two children at play. Water is the joy of the Lord; when He sleeps, it plays that He awaken. And when He awakens, it flows—water does flow. Does it flow?

Yes, but it is not the flow of water. It is the flow of the Lord Himself.

Thunderous now was this flow. Mountains crashed into one another, and the netherworld shook as if gravitation had turned on itself. Men faltered and fell, beasts bellowed. Fear shook the universe. Even Shiva's Parvathi cried out, 'Lord, make not the earth dissolve! The earth still has meaning. Birds have yet to build nests, children have yet to be born. Mankind cannot and must not come to an end.'

Suddenly Shiva, in the midst of his meditation, heard Vishnu laugh. 'Catch the water in your hair,' shouted Vishnu, its waves jumping under His toe. 'Let not so much as a drop fall to earth, for then equinox and orbit will become entangled, and the earth slip up and down like a bubble on a soap-shrub stem.' Shiva quickly caught it in his matted, ages-long hair, and there it would stay, did the water, for a million, million years.

Bhagiratha, who'd foreseen the universe inundated with water and heard the trembling of the green-blue flowing fluid, now heard nothing but the spun silence of the rotating universe. He knew then that neither his sixty thousand ancestors nor the horse would ever be redeemed. Retreating to the inner regions of his being, Bhagiratha wandered like a lost bird. He cried out . . .no response. He wept . . . nobody answered. He prayed . . . nobody appeared. Life remained flat.

In his great love then, Vishnu said, 'Let go the water now—just a little stream, Lord Shiva, no bigger than a woman's braid—that the earth start to grow green again. We, too, need to be prayed to. If the universe of man stopped, what would we do? You and I cannot sleep all the time, nor you in your epic quiet be in meditation.'

There is, however, a secret behind this tale: Mother Parvathi was at the back of it all. Her compassion had sustained the sun and the moon. The roots of plants had not withered, nor had the oxygen of the air corroded; Her wish pulsated the universe. Vishnu's breath was Parvathi's gift. Shiva's meditation was Parvathi's trick. Parvathi alone, Great Goddess, Mother of the world, protects all. She loves play, and She had played with the Lord. And in Her play, the Ganges had descended on the earth. The Vedas sounded again.

But what is Ganges? Ganges is *ap*, water. She starts from Vishnu's toe, swaying and wreathing in the heavens, indifferent to the making or unmaking of space. She flows as she pleases, for who could move movement, or keep water from its quiddity. When she comes to the ethereal mid-regions, she is gentle-flowing *Mandakini*. She attains form to abolish form, goes where she likes, easing the inaccuracies of gods and angels. She ripples and falls through the Milky Way, making planets into playthings of thought. When she flows further down into nether-space, she pours as light onto the top of Mount Meru, lotus-centre of the earth, churning-rod of the ocean.

Shiva having stayed her course, and the heavens and mid-regions containing her strength, she now falls into captivity as numbers, music, forms. Sa becomes *sa, ri* becomes *ri, and then sarigasarigama* to make the manifest note. The universe gathers in her sounds, and music starts its co-relationships. Man's kingdom is saved when sound is in order. Therefore, with each note she becomes a river: *sa* becomes Ganga, *ri* the Jumna, *ga* the hallowed Saraswathi, and *ma* the Narmada, the beloved of the sages. From *pa* comes the Godavari, dear unto Sri Rama; from *dha* the dark Krishna (which united with the Tunga and the Bhadra becomes the Tungabhadra); while *ni* forms the swift little Cauvery, pride of the Pandyan lands.

All the rivers, streams, and rills—thus the raginis—came back into birth to flow through fertile lands. One joined the other, dissolving sound to raise earth to heaven, finally reaching Vishnu's toe . . . then on to Lakshmi's heart itself. Music is river.

The Ganges is the Bhairavi, the Jumna the Malkauns, and so on. The sounds flow to the ocean, vapours rising into sun-clouds to pour over mountains, becoming rivers again that flow down each to her sea. What a play Parvathi created for her own enjoyment. And Shiva danced. Vishnu was so pleased he went back to his epochal sleep.

# Part One

# The Kavis, the Poets

# 1

# The Premiere of Sakuntala

Spring had come to Ujjain in a multiple splendour of flags and flowers, lights and bells. Green grass grew between the cobblestones, and women wore saris the colour of sesamum blossoms. Lights were lit on the eight hills to welcome the Spring god.

In this tenth year of the victory of King Vikramaditya over his foes, kings from Assam, Kashmir, and the Himalayas travelled to Ujjain, along with ambassadors from China, Persia, and Rome, having been sent special invitations asking all to bring with them their most learned men. A great event was to take place in the land this spring.

Kalidasa, his brain having grown dissipated and lain fallow, nevertheless wrote, at seven sittings, a play in seven acts, which was to be performed at the court. The play was a challenge, for as Vikramaditya said, 'If any among you, my kings and ambassadors, has a poet more learned and with more poetry on his tongue, have him come out—and I shall forthwith abdicate in your favour. As great as my prowess and diadem are, great, too, are those who adorn my court.'

Kalidasa, when he heard this, laughed to himself. He knew great kings don't always make for great poets, nor are great poems always done by great poets. True art comes from above, incarnate in magic and word.

He was sleepy the afternoon of the festival. Day after day he had gone to the Court to direct the actors. All had become so stylized in their craft, so practised, that they'd forgotten the simplest art of acting: to give delight. The reigns of great monarchs can in ways be bad, he said to himself; they often produce such arrant buffaloes as these. But he knew there was no changing the actors.

They had objected to this and that. The scene of the fisherman, they said, was perfectly obscene; it went against the holiest tenets of dramatic art. But such vulgarity, Kalidasa had scornfully told them, was necessary. 'We are not always going to speak of kings and queens offering *mandhara* flowers to each other. And pray, dainty lady,' he asked one of the actresses, 'what great Sun-family do you come from? As you know, I am an ox-driver's son.'

The actress playing the part of Priyamvada chirruped to the one acting Anusuya, 'Look, my dear, Kalidasa has gone Sudra!' The professional clown in the play shouted, 'If in our times the sons of ox-drivers make poetry, no wonder children fall from coconut trees!'

Everybody roared with laughter. Reaching for his turban, an angry Kalidasa went straight home, where sleep soon came upon him.

He awoke to the sound of trumpets and still half asleep said, 'Can't the dead be allowed to go to heaven, or hell, in silence? This *noise* . . .'

'No, my boon,' said his servant Menaka, 'it's not a funeral.'

'Then it is a marriage,' said Kalidasa.

'No, the King's men have come. They have brought your *pitambar* and your muslin shirt, and a pair of gold sandals.'

'Send them back!' he muttered.

Going to the door, she said, 'Tell His Highness the poet is very grateful for the gifts.'

'Nothing of the sort!' shouted Kalidasa and in his anger sat up. 'Why must you women always poke into men's affairs? Tell the King that Kalidasa the poet received the King's gift— in his sleep.' He then gruffly dismissed the messengers.

From his bed he could hear the bath-fire purring, see it blazing. He knew it was time to bathe; the attendants were already there with *moghra* oil and scent. He sat down to it patiently, like a little child. Oh, it was good to be soothed by such warmth! He felt glowing thoughts sailing up to his brain; Kalidasa the great poet was to be feted today. Yes, it was a wonderful play, no doubt. But only—well, we'll see how the faces of those bunny-lipped scholars look tonight.

He took his bath quietly, gradually waking from his sleep. Menaka was at the door, holding his new clothes already besmirched with *haldi*. She offered them to him, one by one; he donned them, fold and filigree, with care. After she combed his grey hair back and put on the *tilak* and fitted his earrings, he said, 'Show me the mirror.' He knew he was very handsome.

Forgetting herself, and overcome with gratitude, she kissed him on the lips. Why had he picked *her* as a servant? she wondered. What good karma of the past had earned her this honour? Of course, she was beautiful too, was she not?

He smiled. 'Look, my little butterfly, here comes the chariot.'

As he moved through the evening streets, the clay lamps spluttering with new-lit wicks and the banana festoons hissing against the chariot wheels, gay-decked men and women rode to the Palace in all their finery. A wave of delight unexpectedly swept over him as he thought to himself, 'Something wondrous is happening—but not to me. O not to me, but to this earth.' Deeply moved, he shouted to the charioteer, 'Turn right, and on to the temple!'

'But, Sir,' answered he, reining up. 'His Majesty has already entered the Hall of Pleasaunce, and we should be late if—'

'Slave, obey!' His shout was so commanding, the driver whirled the chariot around, and in a flash they were at Mahakala's Temple. Kalidasa leapt down, and before the priest had time to recognize him, he circumambulated the temple, repeating over and over, 'Great God, it is Yours, it is *all* Yours!'

Performing a rapid camphor benediction, he rushed back to the chariot. By the time its horses strode the cobblestones of the Palace courtyard, the Chamberlain was already there, fuming, then began swearing at the driver. Why had he not brought the poet in time?

Kalidasa, however, he received with festal courtesy, and led him to the Hall of Pleasaunce. Where keen eyes, illumined foreheads, swelling bosoms, and fragrant garlands so welcomed him that he felt compelled to blurt out a lie to the King. 'Sire,' he said, 'I was in the temple, praying. Forgive me, Mahakala kept me.'

The King, who, too, had been nervous but was now at peace, replied, 'When the gods ask, even a King must obey.'

'You are gracious, Sire.'

The drums then struck up the March of Victory, and followed by the courtiers, scholars, priests, ambassadors, and visiting kings, Vikramaditya entered the theatre. Chairs of cane and wood awaited the lesser noblemen, thrones of silver for the kings, and one of gold for Vikramaditya. A low silver ottoman was placed next to him for Kalidasa. The women, already seated, were clad in bright red saris from Benares and peacock-blue ones from Kosala. The queens and princesses were there too. Princess Somaputri greeted Kalidasa with a subtle, knowing simper. And he gave back a mischievous smile.

Princess Somaputri was very beautiful and unmarried. But her stars foretold a widowhood in six months and an orphanhood a year after marriage. So, the King procured for her education the best scholars: Varahamihira, the astronomer; Aryabhata, the lexicographer; and Kalidasa himself, who taught her to write verse.

Sometimes, she and Kalidasa would send each other limericks which concealed much passion on her side and much fun on his. Today, she was very proud; of all those present she alone knew the play. He had read it aloud to her.

And so, the play began.

The actor who played Dushyanta began his part badly. Despite Kalidasa's vehement directions earlier, he made high-flown gesticulations, forgetting that Dushyanta was not an emperor like Vikramaditya but a petty prince visiting a hermitage without his courtiers.

And worst of all, that he was supposed to be in love. Instead of bending down to Sakuntala as if to touch a lotus petal in tenderness, he leapt forward as if thrusting a sword at her. Fortunately, the lighting was not always even, and his errors were unrecognizable to all but the most observant.

On the other hand, Sakuntala—Lalithasena, the courtesan was playing the part—was very well-performed. Lalithasena

was also in love with Kalidasa, and with wide-open eyes had
followed each of his instructions. She was also, unlike our
Dushyanta, highly cultured, who was from the horse guards,
and chosen because he was to play a nobleman only for his
beauty.

But as the play progressed, he seemed to improve and
wasn't too inept when the love scene arrived. Each movement
of hers a melody, he responded to it, quick and supple as a
serpent. Although his exit *was* hurried and clumsy.

In the scene where the King rejected mother and child,
however, they both acted their best; he distant and completely
self-absorbed, playing the just King who could not have
behaved incorrectly, yet still appearing humble. Speaking
with great dignity, he assured her, 'My god, girl, Dushyanta's
conduct is known to the whole kingdom, and nobody would
ever imagine this.' The audience turned to Vikramaditya and
applauded the acting.

Inspired by the applause, Lalithasena, too, outshone
herself, her voice becoming even more vibrant and clear. With
intensity but no tears, walking off the stage she grieved, 'O
Mother Earth, give me a grave!'

Cheer upon cheer arose, and the whole hall stood in
applause, the King throwing flowers on the stage. Returning
to gather the flowers, the actress offered them to the Poet. At
this, everybody cheered Kalidasa.

Only Varahamihari the astronomer did not. He stared at
the lacquered ceiling as though gazing up at birds. He hated all
this fuss, and about what? A man, a king no less, goes hunting
in a forest, sees a hermit's daughter, falls in love with her,
marries her beneath forest-hymen—then abandons her, and
when she comes to him later with his baby, says he does not

even recognize her. Only degenerates and fools could applaud such a thing. Though the King says Hinduism will live again, Varahamihari knew this wasn't how Hinduism would revive. The true object of all action must be *Dharma*. As the ancients said, 'On Dharma does the axle of the Universe revolve.'

'Yes,' he said aloud to no one in particular, 'the play's King is immoral. The *play* is immoral! Look, look at Kalidasa! He needs only a whip in his hand, the ox-driver's son!'

But the play wasn't over; its performers were readying for the next act. Kalidasa was in his seat, resting his chin on his hand. Despite the success of the first act, he was moody, his thoughts far away. For there was a real-life story behind his play.

He was thinking of Her-of-the-forest. That is always how he remembered the girl. Once, long ago on a pilgrimage to the south, still an unknown if ambitious youth, Kalidasa had stopped in the little forest hamlet of Kevala, where he stayed at a ranger's house. The family had adopted a Ghond girl, an orphan, they said, which meant it probably had a story behind it.

In their time together in the forest, he and she had fallen in love, true. But one day, like the poet he was, after many goodly caresses and promises, he bade her good-by. Then, as the months passed, forgot all about her.

Years later, on another journey north, and as the way of Karma will impose, he happened to stop again at Kevala, at the very same ranger's house—except by now Kalidasa the poet was famous, with many chariots and servants in his escort, given him by the kings of the south. When the Ghond girl showed him a child she claimed was his, he did not believe her. In fact, he said he didn't even remember her. Nor could he take on every child that women tried to claim his.

So acting the great man, then the madman, he rejected her and the child and ran away. Yet they'd remained in his mind these last two and thirty years. Now old age was coming. His once-dark curls lay flat in corn-white hair. He was still strong, but in another few years everything would be all but over. Oh, to have a son—a child! Imagine the great Kalidasa without progeny!

His moodiness was violently interrupted by peals of laughter. Gust after gust filled the air, and at first, he thought his audience was mocking him. Instead, people were shouting, 'Again! Once again!' And he relaxed into his seat. Which was when the fisherman came on the stage with the two policemen and their chief.

The policemen strike the fisherman. 'Now, pickpocket, tell us where you found this ring. It's the King's ring, with his name engraved on it and a magnificent gem.'

Frightened, the fisherman cries, 'Be merciful, kind gentlemen. I am not guilty of such a crime.'

First policeman: 'No? I suppose the King thought you were a pious Brahmin and made you a present of it.'

The fisherman: 'Listen. Please. I am a fisherman and live on the Ganges, at the spot where Indra came down.'

Second policeman: 'You thief! We didn't ask you for your social position or your address.' Here the Princess breaks into rippling laughter, and briefly everybody turned towards her.

The fisherman: 'I support my family with the things you catch fish with—nets, you know, hooks and things.'

The chief, laughing: 'My, you have a sweet trade.'

The fisherman: 'Master! Don't say that! You shouldn't put down a lowly trade that your own ancestors began. A butcher butchers animals, and yet he can be the tenderest-hearted of men.'

Chief: 'Go on, go on.'

The fisherman: 'Well, one day I was cutting up a carp. In its maw I see this magnificent ring. That is how I got it, and I was trying to sell it here when you fine gentlemen grabbed me. Now, kill me or let me be.'

Once again, loud applause broke out. The King turned to Kalidasa and told him how remarkable and true the scene was. 'It is good,' he said, 'to ridicule the police; they're always acting *for* kings *against* kings. And I like the way you end it. Let's watch!'

The fisherman: 'Or take half of it, Masters, to pay for something to drink.'

Second policeman: 'Fisherman, you are the biggest and best friend I've got. The only thing we really want is all the brandy we can hold. Let's go now to where they sell it.'

Once again, applause. Only Varahamihira, in consultation with the Princess Somaputri, remained seated. 'It is obscene, Princess, openly obscene. And it pains me to see you praise such a thing.'

'But no, Master, it is truth itself. After all that learned stuff of Bhasa's and Saumille's and Kaviputra's, doesn't it sound true, sound real?'

'Many habits of men, Princess, are true, but we speak of them not. This is not poetry, it is marsh-drama.'

The Princess, however, was not listening. She called to Kalidasa and laughed, 'What a wicked man you are!' Then gave a side glance at Varahamihira. But he was quick with his repartee, and quoting from a previous scene, piped sarcastically, 'Such handsome men are sure to be good, aren't they?'

But Kalidasa, just as quick in retort, answered, 'But the virtuous, Panditji, are rarely blessed by beauty. In fact, I once dreamt of writing a satire after the manner of the Greeks. It was going to be called *Vakrachitra,* or *My Virtuous Ugly Man.*'

The King, following their byplay, broke in. 'And Kalidasa, I knew your hero was going to be an astronomer, was he not? Come, come, you two, don't disturb the listeners.'

In Act VI, after all the fooling of the clown and the fun of archery, when heaven's messenger comes and Dushyanta says, 'My bow is strung; a distant goal calls me, and tasks sublime,' all the nobles applauded and the kings and Vikramaditya bowed to their enthusiasm. But it was when the child was playing with the lion cub and said, 'Open your mouth, cub, I want to count your teeth,' that the women shrieked with laughter, the whole house following suit. The Princess, though, observing Kalidasa, saw a teardrop in his eye.

The movement of the play pulsed, holding the audience. Indeed, spurring them on. So, it was not going to end a tragedy; the King was at last going to see Sakuntala again. And recognizes her. And she accepts him.

> Black madness flies:
>      Comes memory;
> Before my eyes
>      My love I see.
> Eclipse flees far;
>      Light follows soon;
> The loving star,
>      Draws the moon.

Then she cries, 'Victory, vic—.' Her tears choke out the utterance as the poet had written it, Lalithasena playing it well, her hand at her throat, eyes bulging, but a gentle smile on her face. At this, Varahamihira himself stood and applauded when the King's recognition of Sakuntala was explained away by the stars and computations of the past. The moral law of the universe was upheld.

The women, too, were as happy. Bright faces could be seen under jewelled head-serpents, smiling betel-red lips under nose rings. People's gestures grew lighter, and the anklets, bracelets, and toe-rings clinked as though it were a naming-day party at the Palace. When in the play the sage Kanva blessed the pair and their child, many in the audience yearned for a similar blessing for their children. When the sage spoke of the world's coming happiness, all the noblemen cheered, everybody rising for the concluding lines.

> May kingship benefit the land,
>     And wisdom grow in a scholar's band;
> May Shiva see my faith on earth
>     And make me free from all rebirth!

The King himself leapt from his seat, and resting a hand on the Prime Minister's shoulder, the other on Kalidasa's, said so all could hear, 'Ministers, cousins, kings, and my people . . . I have conquered many lands, subdued many enemies, brought paddy where there was poverty and milk where water was scarce. When I am gone, though, neither my conquests nor my plenty will be remembered. But I think, I hope, I beg the very gods that this day will be commemorated—that Kalidasa has written *Sakuntala* in my reign, and it was acted before me.

May Shiva of Mahakal continue to give him strength, and may His Spouse, Parvathi, guide him always.'

'Kalidasa, my cousin and my poet—Gem among the Nine Gems of my Court—herewith I honour thee with this princely shawl.' Whereupon the actors, from the stage, sang a hymn from Act III.

> Vice bends before the royal rod,
> Strife ceases at your kingly nod;
> You are a strong defender.
> Friends come to all whose wealth is sure,
> But you alike to rich and poor
> Are friend both strong and tender.
> Victory to the Victorious! . . .

Outside, the music sounded, and to the astonishment of all, the King himself led Kalidasa to his chariot. The Princess whispered, 'Father, shall I accompany him home? And return?'

Vikramaditya said, 'Of course, my daughter.'

Kalidasa was delighted, as he had no wife to share his honours, no hand-pulling child to be proud of him. And the Princess had always been faithful in praising his play. Hardly had they left the palace gates, the trumpets still sounding, than he took her in his arms and kissed her. She, like the bluestocking she was, responded with words from his own play:

> Her sweetly trembling lips,
> With virgin invitation,
> Provoke my soul to sip,
> Delighted fascination.

Hushing her with a finger to her lips, again he kissed her.

Stopping the chariot at the temple, he had the doors opened and led her inside. A low flame still smoked and smirked, illuminating the idol. Kalidasa told the Princess to ask a question of the god. Straightaway she threw a flower, and cried, 'There! Is not Kalidasa the greatest of poets, and his *Sakuntala* the finest of plays?'

The flower had fallen to the right of the image. From where to both a voice seemed to cry, 'Kalidasa, you have attained the unsurpassable!'

From his bed that night, restless, and nervous even at the rustle of his muslin shirt, he could see the eight lamps of Spring on the eight hills. At the drum of dawn, he lit a lamp and looked into a mirror.

Yes, he had grown old, very old. How vain, how ridiculous are all human attainments—even the unsurpassable. He had done his work; now only the Himalayas remained.

Before the morning's First Audience, he begged the King leave to go on pilgrimage. Vikramaditya, after giving him horses and elephants, jewels and money, shouted from his palace window, 'Come back soon, great poet!'

Kalidasa left the Festival of Ujjain. Never to return.

# 2

# A Nest of Singing Birds

Once upon a time there were two sisters, Aru and Toru Dutt. Toru was eighteen months younger, born on 4 March 1856 at Rambagan. The Dutts of Rambagan were a famous family of Bengal. A branch of them came to Calcutta around the turn of the eighteenth century, their houses rising one beside the other at Maniktola, an older neighbourhood.

Those were the days when people tore pages from books and distributed them to spread, quick and full, the great learning of the West. In Calcutta, they not only discussed international politics, but they also revelled in them; once, Raja Ram Mohan Roy broke his leg, jumping high, when he saw a French flag flying, the flag of liberty. Such was the passion for this new enlightenment that Greek, Latin, Hebrew, French, and German were eagerly studied, many Indian scholars translating these alien texts into their own or other languages, including English. Roy learnt Hebrew and Greek in order to read the Bible in the original and wrote a treatise on Jesus in Persian, with an Arabic introduction.

The Hindu religion, with all its antique, decadent traits seemed confusing and pagan to some. The new learning, however, became associated with the teachings of Jesus himself. Christian missionaries, some of them men of the highest devotion and education, opened colleges in Calcutta—and the fight began between the Anglicists and Orientalists. The Anglicists were convinced that a whole mound of Sanskrit and Arabic books was not worth one of classical European origin, while the Orientalists, though impressed by the mighty impact of this great new world, were not ready to give up the whole Indian tradition because of a few blemishes.

The Dutts of Rambagan, and a whole host of brothers and their wives, would become Christian. Govin Chunder Dutt, at one time a high official under the British and later a Calcutta justice of the peace, was converted with his wife Kshetramohini, so that Toru and Aru were brought up Christians. Their only brother, Ajub, having died earlier, lay buried with a little white cross over his grave.

Aru and Toru lived in Rambagan amidst their cousins and aunts, their learned elders receiving the most distinguished people of Calcutta, Indian and English. They were always looking for more books from Europe and fresh visitors with whom to discuss them. A cultivated Englishman once paid a friendly call on Girish Chunder Dutt, a brother of Govin. 'So,' he asked, impressed by his opulent library, 'what is it you are reading?'

'God,' answered Girish Chunder, 'has denied us children. So, these are our children.' His wife shyly showed their visitor numerous volumes of European classics. At the time, they were reading Schiller.

The Dutts themselves wrote books. Hut Chunder published *Writing: Spiritual, Moral, and Poetic,* and Girish Chunder his *Cherry Blossoms.* Govin, perhaps the most intellectually gifted of all, had published a book of poems and was working on a book of translations from the French and German—later published as *The Dutt Family Album*—in which the poetic gifts of the family found generous expression. One of the more learned Englishmen in Calcutta described Rambagan as 'the nest of singing birds'.

With so enthusiastic, educated, pious, and cosmopolitan a background, it was impossible for Aru and Toru not to be poetic. Their Rambagan house was beautiful, but their country home at Baugmaree was even lovelier. Toru Dutt wrote:

> A sea of foliage girds our garden
> round . . .
> The light green graceful tamarinds
> abound
> Amid the mango clumps of green
> profound,
> And palms arise like pillars grey,
> between . . .
> But nothing could be lov'lier than the
> ranges
> Of bamboos to the eastward, when the
> moon
> Looks through the gaps, and the white lotus
> changes
> Into a cup of silver.

The waters at Baugmaree were full of fish. There were magnificent horses to ride, and such a lot of monkeys. However much these monkeys plundered the garden, it was impossible to shoot them as they had such very human gestures and cries.

Not that it was all idyllic. There were snakes; cows were bitten and sometimes died. As did men in famine, their plentiful death. But Aru and Toru had a protective, tender father.

> I only found
> My father watching patiently by my bed,
> And holding in his own, close-prest,
> my hand.

Like the enlightened Tagores, the Dutts yearned to go to Europe. Theirs would be the first Bengali ladies to cross the oceans, which made it all the more exciting to them. The dream was realized when the family sailed, the mother, father, and two daughters, first to France and then to England. Toru was then thirteen, Aru fifteen.

In France, Aru and Toru went to a *pensionnat* in Nice, where they studied French. In the evenings they would walk along the Promenade des Anglais, where they might see a carnival with its masks and fancy dresses, military trumpets and drums, an astonishing sight for a serious-minded Indian child. They also visited Paris, 'the greatest of all cities,' wrote Govin Chunder, 'in point of beauty, comfort, climate, and cleanliness'. But it was in England the family was to feel most at home.

They reached London in the spring of 1870 and took a house at Brompton. Here they received many friends: Sir George MacFarren, whose wife gave them lessons in music; Sir Bartle Frere, a former Governor of Bombay, cultivated and understanding; and that charming character le Chevalier de Châtelain, a friend of Victor Hugo and well-known translator of Shakespeare's plays. Then there was Sir Edward Ryan, an intimate of Thackeray and Dickens, with whom they discussed Trollope.

'Aru is learning a sonata by Mozart revised by Mr. Pauer,' wrote Toru to Arun, her cousin in Calcutta. 'He is also teaching me *Schmetterlinge*, or *Butterflies*, a very easy, pretty piece.' Later, both sisters went to Cambridge and attended the Higher Lectures for Women, studying French at St. Leonard's. By the time Prussia defeated France in 1870, fourteen-year-old Toru was already writing verse.

> No, she stirs!—There's fire in her
> glance,
> Ware, oh ware of that broken sword!
> What, dare ye for an hour's mischance,
> Gather round her, jeering France,
> Attila's own exultant horde?
>
> Lo, she stands up—stands up e'en now,
> Strong once more for the battle fray,
> Gleams bright the star, that from her
> brow
> Lightens the world. Bow, nations bow,
> Let her again lead on the way!

It was in England that she started her translations of French poets, and many of her unrevealed manuscripts, which she would later bequeath to posterity. She also read *Waverly* by Sir Walter Scott and *Contes et Romans Populaires* by Erckmann-Chatrian.

Tragically, Aru having grown seriously ill—she was coughing and spitting blood—the family had to return to India, but never felt at home there again. They lived with the hope of selling their property, the garden house at Baugmaree, and returning to England. 'We all want so much to see England again,' she wrote to her friend Mary Martin in Cambridge, daughter of the renowned Rev. John Martin, Vicar of St. Andrews the Great. 'We miss the free life we led there. If we ever can fulfil our wish to return to England, I think we shall most probably settle in some quiet country place. The English villages are so pretty.'

But Aru died. 'The Lord has taken dear Aru from us,' wrote her sister to Mary. 'It is a sore trial for us, but His will be done. We know He doeth all things for our good. She left us on the 23rd of July at eleven in the morning, peaceful and happy to the last. She lies beside my brother in our little cemetery beyond the bridge.'

Now only Toru remained. Of her Govin Chunder had written,

> Puny and elf-like, with disheveled
> tresses,
> Self-willed and shy, ne'er heeding that
> I call,
> Intent to pay her tenderest addresses,
> To bird or cat—but most intelligent.

It had been Aru's and Toru's dream to produce a book together, Aru to design the drawings and Toru to write the verse. She'd completed the verses before her death, and the translations from the French poets: some two hundred poems from, among others, Hugo, Lamartine, and Baudelaire. The resulting book was called *A Sheaf Gleaned from French Fields,* published in Calcutta in 1876 with the following introductory verse from Schiller:

*Ich bringe Blumen mit und Früchte*
*Gereift auf einer andern Flur,*
*In einem andern Sonnenlichte,*
*In einer glöcklichern Natur*

*The Indian Charivari, The Madras Standard, The Englishman*, and *The Calcutta Quarterly Review* gave fitting notices of the book, but something quite unexpected happened in England. Edmond Gosse, going one empty day to *The Examiner's* office, was given a shabby little volume by the editor. The postman had just brought it. 'There! See whether you can make something of that,' said the editor. Gosse opened the book, his eyes falling on the lines:

Still barred thy doors! The far east
glows,
The morning wind blows fresh
and free.
Should not the hour that wakes the
rose,
Awaken also thee?

All look for thee, Love, Light, and
Song—
Light in the sky deep red above,
Song in the lark of pinions strong,
And in my heart, true love.

The poem captured him. He was amazed that despite its awkwardness of English style and grammar such verse should come from an Indian and be published at the *Saptahiksambad Press* at Bhowanipore. 'When the history of the literature of our country,' he wrote a few years later, 'comes to be written, there is sure to be a page in it dedicated to this fragile, exotic blossom of song.' When André Theuriet wrote about her in the *Revue des Deux Mondes*, Toru at once became famous. The post brought her letters which bespoke her fame, and poets sent her their books, notably *Au Poète, an hommage* by Auguste Faure. The slender volume was addressed '*À* Toru Dutt, *Poète*'.

Meanwhile, Toru had caught the same cough as Aru. She, too, began to lose weight and spit blood. It was time to sell the Baugmaree house and sail for Europe; the Engadine valley in Switzerland, they said, was wonderful for failing breath. The house, however, could not be sold. Between cough and fever, Toru continued to work on her Sanskrit and poems, producing a collection titled *Ancient Ballads and Legends of Hindusthan.* Coming down the staircase became more and more difficult.

She read voraciously. Books, fortunately, came to her frequently—from Hachette, for instance, the *Dictionnaire of Monsieur Littré*, in four volumes; *Son Excellence M. Eugène Rougon*; and *Les Misérables.* She had not read *Madame Bovary* or Daudet's works but hoped to soon.

Wrote Govin Chunder, thinking of his daughter:

> *Que faut-il pour être heureux comme*
> *dans le pays des fables?*
> *Une chaise, deux chats, et Les Misérables!*

Toru was also a great admirer of Victor Hugo. She translated his magnificent discourse at the French Chamber of Deputies in 1851, which was published in *The Bengal Magazine*.

But she continued to spit blood. She was now working on *Bianca, or The Young Spanish Maiden*, a prose romance, while touching up another novel in French, *Le Journal de Mademoiselle D'Avers*. Both are autobiographical pieces, in which the young die noble and virtuous, with a firm faith in Providence. Though Toru never stopped longing for England, suddenly she grew gravely ill and died. '*Dieu nous aie en sa garde*', her character Mademoiselle D'Anvers had prayed. '*Elle ferma les yeux; ses lèvres s'entr'ouvrirent, et son âme pure s'envola par là vers le sein de son Dieu, et Marguerite s'endormit du sommeil de la mort.*'

But as one small light had flickered out, another had been lit, one that was to prove a major illumination for Bengal and for India. In Jorasanko, 'that great rambling mansion in the heart of Calcutta's teeming life', and not far from Rambagan, was born Rabindranath Tagore on 6 May 1861. The Dutts of Rambagan were both neighbours and compeers of the Tagores. *Bhan Songs*, the first work of Rabindranath, was printed in 1877, a year after the publication of Toru's *A Sheaf Gleaned from French Fields*.

In 1879, in Paris, Mademoiselle Clarisse Bader, a kindly French Orientalist, brought out Toru's *Le Journal de Mademoiselle D'Arvers*. She would come to be compared to George Sand and George Eliot. James Darmesteter praised her for the sobriety of her writing, and Andre Desprex for its freshness and idyllic quality. *Ancient Ballads and Legends of Hindusthan*, her most mature work, was published in 1882 in London. Edmond Gosse wrote a memorial and concluded it with these lines:

Thy generous fruits, though gathered
ere their prime,
Still showed a quickness, and maturing
time
But mellows what we write to the dull
sweet of Rime.

# 3

# The Poet

The world was young then. It was between the two world wars. The Lake of Geneva rippled with its grey-green waters. Across it you could see Mount Blanc, the white, shimmering snow on top like a garland of sacred hyacinth on Shiva's head.

I was young, too, twenty-years-old, perhaps twenty-one. The year was 1930. I could almost see Shiva and Parvathi playing chess on the mountain heights at Kailas. The Indian carries his Himalayas everywhere, and his Ganges; the world seems constantly at play, and you play along with it. India itself, remember, is *lila*, play.

Along the lake, on the farther side, was Vevey, where the great Romain Rolland lived. He had just completed his two books on Ramakrishna and Swami Vivekananda. His tribute to Gandhi had been published years earlier, the first book of its kind to be written in Europe. I once visited Rolland, carrying my copy of *Jean Christophe,* one of the most famous European novels of the era—a young book for a very young man. Rolland looked a monk, clad all in black with piercing, pain-covered eyes, yet they'd shown with both concern and compassion for the young man who'd come calling. Though he seemed youthful himself, he also looked medieval in the longing in his face for God.

Annie Besant was in Geneva, too, but not Krishnamurti, who was at his own camp in Holland. He had finally broken with the Theosophical Society, unwilling anymore to be seen as its 'Messiah of this Age'. But Col Leadbeater, who had long ago chosen him the new Christ, was visiting Geneva at the time for an international conference of the Society. Having a reputation for perceiving a person's stellar destiny, he thought perhaps I, too, was meant for some apostolic future. He had once predicted a cousin of mine would be one of the future companions of the messianic Krishnamurti, but this cousin died prematurely at Oxford during the infamous global flu epidemic. The stars have their own game, you know.

One afternoon I was invited to a magnificent luncheon by a rich, very rich American who had also come to the Theosophical Conference in Geneva. This tall, handsome man, with his lovely, short wife, wanted to adopt me—maybe a starry trick of Leadbeater's? —but having a father already, I refused to be the son of another.

Life is bright when one is young, the trees greener—the wonder is there's so beautiful a world at all. Youthful limbs have the itch of leaps, the *dhoti* covering them fluttering in the wind. In Geneva I wore a dhoti, contemplating the high snows under the silvery sunshine. How blessed to be in Geneva on *Lac Léman* at age twenty!

I would walk the streets by the lake in solitude, enjoying the wind as it played with the waters and the tall *chêne* trees. The universe turns on its pivot, whirling, knowing it alone exists, while man walks counting time, step by step, as sure as Calvin on the hard pavements of Geneva. Somewhere far away, on the other side of the lake, was the impressive white building of the League of Nations. The League was created that the world see no more war, and men and women believed in it, wholly, assuredly.

But *I* walked forsaken, and alone; I saw no Indians anywhere, everyone was white, and as a provincial Brahmin I never spoke to strangers. Despite the beauty of those green days, I walked in solemnity. The world was the white man's then, and to him, fair and perfect. One had to accept this, for that was the truth of things.

Then came Tagore, Rabindranath Tagore, *the* poet of the world. People have forgotten, but back then, when one said 'poet', he meant Rabindranath Tagore, however difficult it was to pronounce his name.

Alive with the eagerness of youth, yet feeling an outsider, one day I walked into a compound surrounding a great mansion, a young man from nowhere, who immediately felt at home as never before in Geneva. With a dhoti swishing round my limbs and a silken *kurta* falling to my knees, in full summer shine I approached Tagore's Swiss Jorasanko—the mansion of the great man, the Poet, the *Kavi* of the Rig Veda—and into India at last. Unintroduced and brave, I went inside and became, in an instant, one of his large household.

There were so many, many Indians there, I felt at home. I'd entered the realm of the beautiful Kavi in awe, with silent footsteps, for I knew he was there, his presence shining everywhere. It was like being in a king's palace, with a chamberlain, waiters, visitors, and offerings—or in the celestial abode, the *Vaijayanta* of Indra. No questions were asked, no one inquiring who I was or where I came from. I stepped in here and walked out there, where I discovered the poet at his table, happy as happiness itself, smiling, laughing, even joking at times. I sat before him a *chela,* a pupil of the elder.

The Reverend C.F. Andrews—a saint if ever there was—joined us at the table, sitting before *his* rishi, too, his God. In his eyes and mine, never could you meet any man as handsome, as divine as Rabindranath Tagore.

'You know, sir,' said the English clergyman in passing to the poet, 'there were some south Indian boys recently who came to visit your Santiniketan. They said they were penniless, so we fed them.'

'And what did they do then?' asked the poet mischievously.

'Oh! They walked through the whole of Santiniketan, hushed, hands folded, as if it were a place of pilgrimage, a Krishna Vrindavan.'

'Then what happened?'

'They were good boys, very good boys. We were pleased to have them there. They missed you though, sir.'

'And then?'

'They left.'

'*How* did they leave?' asked the poet.

'All joyous and happy, but sad, too,' said the Reverend. 'Sad that they'd missed seeing you.'

'I see', said Tagore with a teasing smile on his broad, pink face. 'But, Charlie, are you sure they did not have more money in their pockets when they left than when they came?'

'Oh, no!' laughed this Charles Andrews, this good clergyman. 'They only came in the hope of paying you their respects. As I said, that you weren't there disappointed them terribly.'

At the poet's insinuation, light-hearted as it was, being a boy myself I felt a little discomfort. But it passed quickly. I knew his remarks were not meant for me; I had a Government of Hyderabad scholarship and some money in my pocket.

The gods had been kind. And if ever I had seen a god, it was indeed Rabindranath Tagore.

One afternoon at tea, Tagore spoke to his guests in such self-absorption it was as if he were talking to himself. It was a desperately true moment. Outside, the afternoon was bright, the Alps filling the sky, the Rhone flowing near. I was so awed I slipped into silence, and being young, remained there. Silence is a form of worship; age and beauty and nobility give you a sense of no time. Before the godlike Tagore, you could only offer yourself like a chant or hymn rising to a sound that is no sound. It was good to be twenty, an age of space and no time, for distance creates intimacy.

Tagore, being a poet, spoke as if words had no vibrance, only meaning; again, he was *the* poet. I didn't fully realize this until Tagore addressed his guests over tea. 'In Germany,' he began, 'I saw, as I travelled the countryside, people standing on both sides of the railway lines holding flowers. They cheered and sang, treating me like a king. The country was beautiful, with green, primeval forests and vast rivers, as if one were back in the time of the Vedas, when the Aryans first arrived in India. It reminded me of Viswamitra's Vedic hymn to the rivers, the earth opening itself like a gift to man—green, fresh, soft.

'So too was it in Italy,' he continued, 'India being an enchanting name abroad. Mussolini, you know, had invited me there. The castles, the cathedrals, the hills were filled with history and sunshine—time sparkled as I moved. I loved the people. I love all people. I worship man.

'It was the same in South America . . . I cherished the people in those countries too. I went there at the invitation of the Chilean poet Pablo Neruda. In comparison with those of Europe the people of South America look ancient; in many ways they seem our kin. The waters ran broad and wild, with man silent. Walking through its forests, one sees that man is a magical gift of God.'

On another afternoon, again over tea, Tagore spoke poetry. It was beautiful to hear his silver-tongued voice, it sounding so grave and wise. Beauty articulated, his poetry shone in whatever he said or did. As his man is a gift of God, he seemed a gift to mankind. Again and again he said, 'I love man,' as if speaking of Primal Man, He who precedes creation. This reminded me of the Purusha Suktha in which Primal Man, if you'll remember, is sacrificed by the gods to create the universe.

Returning to the South American people, he then said, 'In the remote past, I was told, on a high altar they sacrificed a chosen man to their God. It was as if God were sacrificing Himself to Himself. And isn't that what this beautiful earth is about? It is a mirror for man to see himself. Worship, so say the Vedas, is just that: Man "seeing" Himself, thus there is no one there, all the world a temple. That is Truth.'

Then one day, the whole mansion fell into a great commotion. I was wandering through the corridors when I found everybody excited about celebrating some event. A great event, they said. I embraced their excitement, for an Indian at my age expected to see the gods everywhere. When in Rabindranath Tagore's presence, you are neither on this earth, flat and solid, nor in the heavens, but in the high Himalayas. Until you know Tagore—a *Rajarishi*, a royal sage in

the court of the gods—you cannot conceive of a Viswamitra.
Or a Vasistha.

Suddenly, the household fell silent. Everybody ran to his
room, and after a while the men reappeared in black suit and
tie, the women in their finery. It was as if they were going to
a European party for some dignitary, say, at the Government
House in Madras. Though nobody wore medals, everyone
looked statesmanlike.

As for me, it being dinnertime, I was overcome with
hunger and in need of quick-found food. I rushed to the
kitchen, where I saw many biscuits and rich cakes on a tray.
There was no one around but the cooks, who, sensing my
hunger, kindly gave me a piece of cake.

I swallowed it hurriedly, and after washing my face at the
kitchen sink and collecting my dhoti fringe, I rushed toward
the mansion's main door. Upon passing Tagore's bedroom,
I beheld something enchanting. He stood before a mirror
combing his hair, concentratedly, slowly, with a nobility that
seemed almost ancient. He always impressed one as being
ancient, from an age of a thousand years ago. Yet also real,
a person of his time, as a sage should be. His silken, flowing
garments were well-tailored, with flowering gold at the edges
like a brocade. His hair shone white with wisdom.

As I watched him, he turned and smiled warmly, looking at
me with an almost paternal compassion. Stung at being caught
in the act of spying on him, I fled toward the main door, where
a friend, René Andres, greeted me. After I shared what had
happened, he offered both concern and protection. God protects;
there is always protection for the innocent and the brave.

Outside, the afternoon sunshine poured on the motherly
earth. It was midsummer, with perhaps a hint of autumn.

From the door, I could see an array of distinguished-looking people gathered on the front lawn, seated on stiff chairs. A man standing by me said, 'Do you know, young man, who they are?'

'No, sir.'

'Members of the Committee of Intellectual Cooperation of the League of Nations. They have come to pay homage to the poet.' Hearing this, I felt my eyes well with tears.

Just then, from behind us, striding the long, carpeted corridor came Rabindranath Tagore. Tall and majestic he was, handsome and noble, not unlike a statue of a Greek god at the museum in Geneva. A high black cap adorned his head like a royal priest's crown. Upon his reaching the stage, the whole assembly of some fifty or sixty stood to honour him. Appearing next to him a moment later was none other than Albert Einstein, who then began a short if magnificent speech only an Einstein could have given.

At its close, Tagore bowed low to the assembly. Absolute silence followed; the earth stood still, the air seeming to whisper the whisper of the lily. Taking it all in, he knew as he bowed that the homage was not being paid to him but to his India.

It was good I'd worn a dhoti, for I felt as if I were at a religious festival back home. Mount Blanc felt it, too, I could tell.

Rabindranath Tagore left for Soviet Russia the very next day.

# 4

# Trois Écrivains Universels

Three writers in the last sixty years could perhaps be called *écrivains universels*: Leo Tolstoi, Romain Rolland, and Albert Camus.

Rabindranath Tagore, of course, is acclaimed by many as the greatest writer since Byron. He lived freely, and in a more spacious time, until his eightieth year. Though he was fifty when Tolstoi died, he does not seem to resonate well with contemporary readers. Whereas Tolstoi did not merely catch the mood of the times—which Tagore did, too, as his popular works predating the Great War contained strong motifs of lotus and dawn, peacock and moonlight—Tolstoi lives on. Even today, he is perhaps the most read writer in the world; without doubt, the most read foreign writer in India. Maybe in all of Asia.

Romain Rolland was a direct spiritual successor to Tolstoi. In fact, Rolland, still a young man, wrote to Tolstoi expressing his deep feelings of love and respect for the master. He also wrote a book on the life of the great man, and later a biography of Mahatma Gandhi, probably the most famous disciple of Tolstoi's. Thus did the curve turn on itself and become a circle.

Albert Camus, though not an intellectual heir of Tolstoi, was certainly a spiritual successor to Rolland. He possibly influenced the world more than any of his contemporaries. Why? Because he doubted doubt. And in doing so, turned to India.

But why didn't Dostoevski, according to me a more profound writer than Tolstoi, attain the same universal significance? And why not Andre Gidé, a more authentic craftsman than Romain Rolland? For what reason did André Malraux, an incomparably greater writer than Camus, as Camus himself declared, not outshine his self-admitted inferior? Or for that matter, why did Tagore fall short, who in a world of nationalistic exaltations spoke with such nobility of the man universal? He even founded a university, Santiniketan for the universal man.

The answer is simple: we live in a moral age—and may just be entering into a metaphysical one. This explains Camus. Industrial civilization, having broken the inhibitions of tradition, threw mankind into a universe of multiple confusions of race and caste, religion and non-religion. During the time of the British, the Russians, and, of course, the French of the Republic, the moral man was awakened. Imperialism fares ill with intelligence on the rise.

This breaking down of barriers, however, left man gasping. He had never seen so much space in front of himself. But time grew contracted. The compression between the space-element and the time-instinct created fear in a world suddenly spotted with railway stations. He had to have something to hold on to; a universal religion had to be created, and Dostoevski was too Christian to be universal. Tolstoi, on the other hand, was a Christian who felt Christ an equal of the Buddha, Confucius, and Mohammed.

Rolland, essentially a child of the Christian tradition, wrote of Ramakrishna and Vivekananda. Camus recoiled from Marxism, a divisive creed, to socialism and fair play. He left Sartre to do justice to history, and Andre Malraux to look beyond history. Hence, where metaphysics and religion often divide man, upholding the moral principle behind each makes one immediately universal. This explains why Tolstoi, except for the authors of holy books, is perhaps the more extensively read writer.

We must also remember that the only other author with Tolstoi's universality was Victor Hugo. He is still, after Tolstoi, the most popular foreign writer in Asia. People read *Resurrection* first, then went on to *Les Misérables*, the state of *la misère* being the keynote of Asian nationalism. Not a '*misère*' of want, but of stupor—then the fall into chaos. The Japanese intellectuals of the Meiji era and the Indians of the Victorian era were overwhelmed by the splendour of the European way of life. Not only, they thought, had the machine come—that mighty, whirling, and puffing new god—but also Christ, who arrived after the machine.

Madhusudhan Dutt, a great poet of Bengal, wrote in English, learnt Greek, Latin, French, and German, but thought he could not be a fully accomplished modern man unless he became a Christian. Upon converting to Christianity, he became Michael Madhusudhan Dutt. Tokutomi Roka, the Japanese writer, characteristically enough went to Jerusalem, and from there to Tolstoi's former home, Iasnaia Poliana. Tagore's younger brother bought a steam ship with which to ply the waters of the Ganges. He thought if you could own and run a steamship—he could not—you could conquer the world like the British or French. A young Mohandas Gandhi, from a family strictly vegetarian for centuries, briefly tried eating meat; he felt the strength of the British came from beef. He would give it up, though, along with his Christian leanings and go back to vegetarianism and the Gita.

At this moment of confusion in Asian life and outlook, Tolstoi appeared. As a vegetarian, he castigated the eating of meat. As a Christian, he said that in every individual a spiritual element is manifested that gives life to all that exists. This spiritual element, he believed, strives to unite with everything of a like nature to itself and attains its aim through love. Not confined to Christianity, the same concept can be found in certain tenets of Hinduism, Judaism, Mazdaism (the teachings of Zoroaster), Buddhism, Islam, Taoism, Confucianism, and the writings of the Greek and Roman sages.

In a letter to a Hindu revolutionary, Gandhi reiterated Tolstoi's concept of the spiritual element. Which became, in fact, one of the great forces behind nationalist India. Recalling Ramakrishna, and before him Raja Ram Mohan Roy (who had learnt Greek and Hebrew to write a life of Jesus, then turned to the Upanishads for light), nationalist India denounced Christianity—the religion of the rulers—and fought back with her own traditions. When a Western writer such as Tolstoi (to the Asian, Russia is also a part of the West) decried the horrors of Christianity but not of Christ, and spoke of Krishna and Buddha with reverence, he became a part of the 'everyman's' heritage.

Even Shakespeare, that great bard of Avon, as the Englishman never ceased repeating to the Indian—even he acted as a cog in the wheel of imperialism. With Shakespeare and the Christian canon of the Bible, the British empire would last forever.

Tolstoi, that *other* bard, wrote against Shakespeare. Not only was he vegetarian—already a Hindu of sorts—and an admirer of the Buddha, Krishna, Confucius, and Muhammed, he attacked Shakespeare. Thus did Tolstoi become a *rishi*, a sage. Later, Romain Rolland was also called a rishi by the good Indians.

This historical mood might well have come and gone, as many such periods before and after, but for one important event that shook Asia to its very depths: the war between Russia and Japan, between the powerful West and the traditional East. Japan defeated Russia, which according to the Asians meant the East had won forever. Asian nationalism was born—and at about the same time, before the gates of the Winter Palace, Bolshevism.

From 1905 up to the beginning of the Great War, Tolstoi was perhaps the world's most recognized figure, the first author to attain such significance. Neither Plato nor Aristotle, Shakespeare nor Dante, had influenced mankind in so large a measure and deep a manner. Tolstoi was a moralist, not a metaphysician, a fighter not a mystic; he worked as it were horizontally not vertically. He created an *emotional* mood in India—in all of Asia—not an artistic or intellectual one. The artist was, therefore, lost in the prophet, or in general, as he himself said, 'Corrupt stupidity termed art'. The author of *Anna Karenina* and *War and Peace* was hardly known in Asia, but the writer of *Resurrection* and *What Then Must We Do* became famous. The West was defeated, and hurrah to the East!

A most pertinent question for history to ask is, if the Russo-Japanese War had never been, or if Russia had won, would Dostoevski have prevailed over Tolstoi? India produced no *War and Peace,* though it could have after the famous Sepoy Mutiny of 1857, which somewhat resembled in its circumstances Napoleon's invasion of Russia, with the Mogul emperor the czar. Nor did it produce Dostoevski's *The Possessed,* even though India had many Shatovs, with Indian revolutionaries actually coming to Paris to learn the making of bombs from Russian terrorists. Madame Cama even sold her beautiful, long hair to have enough money to learn bomb-making.

But in the end, Gandhi won against Tilak, Tolstoi against Dostoevski. As today Camus supersedes Malraux.

But as a writer, indeed one of the great novelists of all time, Tolstoi has little or no influence in Asia today. When one looks at the books of Western authors translated into Asian languages—Fénelon, Defoe, Milton, Goethe, even Shakespeare—Tolstoi is one of the least represented. His novels did have some vogue in Japan with the *Shirakasa* school, but in India the only writer who seems influenced by Tolstoi the artist is Rabindranath Tagore. His *Home and the World*, which deals with the dual emotions of a married woman, might have emerged from *Anna Karenina.* One of the paradoxes of history is that what seems to succeed—the new, the revolutionary— actually fails, not by sabotaging its newness, its ideology, but by absorbing heresy into orthodoxy, the moral flowing into the metaphysical.

What is universal in art is orthodoxy, referring man always to the Truth within. The moralist inevitably dies, concerned as he is, not with the Truth but the world. Has not Gandhiji said, 'I once thought God was Truth. Now I think Truth is God.' God then becomes the sacrificial victim of man; *Satyaméva jayate*, Truth alone triumphs. Tolstoi the moralist, the ideologist, influenced Asia deeply, historically. The climate of Asia, so far as it was imbued with an anti-West moral bias, fed on some form or other of Tolstoism. Biryukov succeeded in Asia, but not Tolstoi; Tolstoism succeeded against Tolstoi the artist.

Tolstoi has yet to be rediscovered by Asia. Ivan Karamazov, understanding 'The Grand Inquisitor', must ultimately feel the younger brother of Alyosha Karamazov, not the older. The end of Camus may become the beginnings of a metaphysical Tolstoi, the *écrivain universel*. Goethe discovered Kalidasa. Unless the word and meaning become one, like Parvathi and Parameshwara, there could be no Vyasa, the great chronicler of war, of and within man.

Tolstoi, like his Anna, died in a railway station.

# 5

# Gunter Grass: Cat and Mouse

Some years ago, many writers had written off the novel, born as it was of a certain air of leisure, psychological subtlety, and gracious living—imagine a Balzac or Gide without gracious living.

In these days of speed and destruction, of half-understood statements made at inappropriate moments (no moment being appropriate, for all of them are hurried), they asked, 'How can you sit and plod through E. M. Forster when you can look at picture books?' Easy to read and educative to page through, even if the text does turn out tough, they say something you can understand. They have the intensity of the life you actually lead, like the moment you open a book between boarding suburban trains or underground cars.

E. M. Forster was the only optimist among these writers. He said the new novel will be poetical; I wish he had said metaphysical, but that would not be Forster's language. Between Hitler's war and the Marxist intellectual debacle (inclusive of Sartre's existentialist humanism), the world gained a new perspective. It disapproved of the solidity of the solid-seeming world so dear to the eighteenth-century philosophers, but which both Rimbaud in poetry and Cezanne in painting destroyed before modern physics confirmed their nihilistic apprehensiveness.

And of course, the novel, as it were, went the way of the solid-seeming world. But storytelling is as old as man and whether you tell a story to state or hide a thing, a story will be told. There could even be a story saying there *was* no story.

One such novel is the *Cat and Mouse* of Gunter Grass. A young German writer of immense dexterity in dealing with all materials—human beings and objects—he possesses a rare power of imagination that dispenses swift if ambiguous statements.

In this, his second novel—the first his remarkable *The Tin Drum*—he speaks of boys going to school and growing up in the war of their fathers, beguiled by the glories of the army. But their adventures on a Baltic beach have to do with immediate objects: a sunken Polish mine sweeper in the harbour, monuments to heroes, and boys going to girls as naturally as to any object. The act of thinking seen as an object, too.

In fact, this is a book about objects. The young student Mahlke, after learning to swim, becomes a fanatical diver, retrieving relics from the rusted minesweeper, their 'barge'. Though he became the Great Mahlke to the boys, he cared only for the Virgin Mary. He alone of the boys swims into the submerged mine sweeper, farther and farther, until discovering the former radio hutch, a clammy yet mostly dry room left protruding above the water. Here he builds himself a sort of chapel. Around his neck, he wears a spanner he found in the boat as a cross.

He worships the Virgin Mary. He does not know God. When he gets older and goes into the army, he returns a hero, but his former headmaster refuses to let him address the students of the school. While a student, Mahlke had once stolen a renowned guest speaker's military cross.

The rejected Mahlke strikes the headmaster's face, 'left right with the back and palm of his hand'. Ultimately, in supreme terror at what he'd done, he flees to the radio hutch—the Virgin's chapel. Gulls come and sit on his discarded boots. He never surfaces.

He left objects behind to enter into silence. The headmaster would die amid objects.

# 6

# Thumboo's Krishna

There are only two real perspectives on existence, one that is human, the other abhuman. The first is that of *dukkha* (as preached by the Buddha), 'the sorrow of the sorrow that *sorrow* be'. The second, the *abhuman*, is that of the impersonal, the Truth of Krishna, *ananda*, joy, beyond agony and ecstasy, the play of the pure non-dual. In the human, it's the prince Gautama leaving his newborn child and young wife behind in the palace to seek the Truth. In the abhuman, it's Krishna dancing with the *gopis*, 'sporting with them all, He sported but with one'.

To contrast them further, Krishna, also a prince, leads the Pandavas, His cousins, into battle. While the Buddha is *in* existence (the seventy-two elements of the self, etc.), Krishna, as essence, pure beingness, is *beyond* existence. By stripping oneself of the illusory self—the attributes of the person, hence the persona—one reaches the Buddha's *nirvana*.

But when Krishna is the charioteer directing the battle of life, He is beyond duality, at each moment not he, but *It*. For to go beyond the human, the existential, is to be Purusha, the universal being who is no person, but Truth itself. It is a complex proposition, but Truth has to be One, rather the One-not-two—and so *It*.

This complexity has been chanted in India by many, many poets. For to the Indian, the poet is the *Kavi,* the Sage, the one who lives the non-contradictory event, or Reality. Each *gopi*—and every human is a gopi—perceiving the world, dances the Word in its every perception. And in so doing, forgets himself and becomes the dance. There is no dancer but Krishna.

To achieve this centrality of experience, and even more to express it, requires the vision of a real poet. Edwin Thumboo has touched this truth in his poem entitled 'Krishna'—a rare achievement today, I think. For to concretize the non-dual in the dual is indeed pure poetry.

And here, poetry is wisdom.

* * *

## Krishna

For Raja Rao, by Edwin Thumboo

Before he became a god
To tidy up the world, Krishna
Searched a thousand years,
Along the peaks, the lesser hills,
Each sudden plain, persistent star,
The columns of his thought,
Down deeply anxious limbs
His great inclines of heart

To the rim of the world at sunset . . .
Searched among the maidens of the day,
The maidens of the night,
A face for Bindavan.


Under her consequential sun,
The computations of very rising moon,
That face grew, asserted
All his love, his dreams
Softly magical, destinations.
She gazed upon him
With a look of morning lotus,
Till each stood within the other.
So the blue god, his votive flute
Multiplying his love, the gopis,
Sporting with them all,
He sported with but one.


Perched upon a chord of time,
His yearning flute unfolds
The lovely burden of her eyes
To feed his nimble fingers.
Within the radiance of each note
So bound to her answering look,
The world revives, quickens,
Renews itself, turns whole,
Adores their love unparalleled.
And so they sit, ever moving,
Ever still, in stone,
In ivory, in us.

# For Brother Thumboo

by Raja Rao

Poetry in essence is multi-meaninged,
Overreaching the sound to
The core of silence, wherein
One lives in lucidity, unknowing
There ever was death. The
End is false, for space
Has no beginning, and man
Has only to speak
Poetry—being alone.

Thus Krishna,
Brother Thumboo's name
Of Truth, the
Many gopis,
Each as each,
And Krishna
Each within each
The singular word.

The Absolute never
Fails the thread of song.
Poetry is born
On the lone tongue of Truth,

So that each vocable
Dances without

Movement, for
Krishna dances
Meaning.

Is that not so, Brother Thumboo?

# 7

# Braj Kachru

Braj Kachru is like the areca palm, thin, tall, head held high, his hair spreading out like leaves, curved and crenulated like those of the areca.

His hands spread out, too, like a pandit's hands, fingers meek and long, as if wearied by the counting of beads, *rudraksha* beads. His ancestors, for two or three millennia, moved from bead to bead, uttering the various nomenclatures of Shiva—Shiva the dancer, Shiva of the crematorium, Shiva of the meditation who will not open His eyes.

These pandit ancestors of Braj, too, must have had their eyes closed, trying to see their Shiva, rememorating His virtues, Him ascetic and bare, beating His drum and making the fundamental sounds of alphabets, their vowels and consonants—the long vowels the pandit Kachrus must have enounced, round and deep, to make the vibrations touch their very being. From these ancients, Braj has inherited his soft speech, his slow, guttural elisions, that Shiva might be pleased, His language dancing out the world and inhalating it, so that time dies at each breath. Consequent to which, grammar is born.

Grammar, indeed, not just of the nouns, pronouns, and verbs, but the complexities of levels at which sound arises and meaning be seen as coexistent with it. Making birth and death one, like the universe itself. So is it, too, with beauty and love.

If you should meet Braj anywhere, in Delhi or Illinois, you'd come face to face with a man not of our time but of three thousand tall, rounding years ago. Why so ancient, you ask? That is how a Kashmiri Brahmin is made, inheritor of Abhinavagupta's and Jayaratha's *Shaiva Siddhanta*, one of the profoundest philosophies of mankind—and its secret, its very secret and magical epiphany of the marriage of vowel and consonant. Which dissolves truths of different depths and the concrete world itself, all receding by final dissolution into the Truth. For remember, and remember always, Shiva is Truth. *Shivoham, Shivoham*: 'I' am Shiva. And so, dance.

The last time I saw Braj was on the campus of the University of Oklahoma at Norman, and he seemed to walk as if *he* was dancing. As he was with Edwin Thumboo of Singapore, half-Chinese and half-Indian, they seemed to dance together, like vowel and consonant. I and my wife Susan stood and watched them perform the dance of soundless sound, sounding.

To understand Braj, that great linguist of non-native speakers of English (speaking or writing), you must perforce know something of the complexities of the Word, *Vac,* which his ancestors bequeathed to him. If he bewilders you with his scholarship, you must never forget the millennia of work gone into his blood, which has given him his dexterity of mind and choreobatics of body.

To understand him, you must know the secrets of Vac, the Word, which Kashmiri Shaivism has analysed, and the deep effectivity of the resonant word. As the Vedas say, it is Vac which created the universe—thus the vowel and the consonant, and the four levels of the vocable: the vulgar; the middle levels; the ideational; and the supreme *Para Vac*, which is, of course, the Absolute.

And that is Shiva. Never forget it's His drum that created the alphabet, the play of the soft and hard sounds, the vibrations of destruction and of grace that make for the movements of the Dance. After all, Shiva dances not *to* time, but *on* time, to kill time, the objective world. And in this killing is—meaning.

There is a theory that the Vedas came from Kashmir, the land of Saraswathi, the Goddess of Learning. To understand Braj Kachru, his height and depth, you must go back to the Vedas, to Abhinavagupta and Jayaratha. Should you understand him, *truly* understand him, you will experience awe, accompanied by a deep withdrawal into yourself.

For you will have seen the Shiva in him, where word and meaning are One. There will be no Braj, but only He.

# 8

# Tagore: Renaissance Man

Handsome as a god, indisputable in his greatness, Tagore seems to be the Prophet of the Plains rather than the Shiva of the Mounts:

In the northern region, there is a supreme mountain ruler
of divine essence, named
Himalaya. Immersed in the ocean to the
east and to the west, he rises to serve,
shall we say, as a unit of measure for the earth.

Kalidasa

Translation by Raja Rao and Mireille Chapelle

From a boat on the Ganges, he made his floating nest. And he sings. Too much perhaps: more than a thousand poems, two dozen plays, three thousand songs, eight novels, so many short stories. One sings because of the Silence; one does not sing the Silence. 'Silence is the predication of the Absolute,' said the great fourth-century sage, Shankaracharya.

God couldn't be river without the ocean. Benares, as well, is not on the Ganges: the Ganges *is* Benares. Tagore strolled its banks but made no pilgrimages there: he is indeed that prophet of the plains where men live. Listen to Tagore sing:

> The worshipper offers leaves and fruit to the river, and
> completes his worship.
> Thus, I fill the basket and offer songs to the Ganges,
> water of life.
> And also, I worship Her.

Translation by Raja Rao and Mireille Chapelle

The century had matured when Tagore entered the world. 'I was born in 1861,' he wrote in an autobiographical essay, 'a date of little importance for world history, but crucial to the history of Bengal.' This was also the time of Lamartine, Tennyson, and Whitman. The glory of the world and its 'new man' were being sung everywhere. Glory to the new man who made big heroic things, big mechanical things, big universal things. And glory to God who created humanity.

*Man* is the greatest discovery of nineteenth-century India, as it was for sixteenth-century Europe. Gods were known, of course, but man was somewhat forgotten. There were too many gods and too many priests—not enough men of gods. Vishnu, Shiva, Rama, or Krishna, divinities seemed watered-down into rites as rivers vanish among the desert sands. God had become an empty display of learned gestures.

Then came the British.

Boats arriving from the west brought us conquerors and took back spices and muslins. Others came and brought Baptists and Methodists, more rarely an engineer, an apothecary (Keats had planned to open an herbalist shop in Madras), an educator—

who spoke neither of Socrates nor Spinoza, but of Locke and Hume, and even of Jeremy Bentham. Steamboats went up the Ganges. The West was victorious. Victorious because of its machines, of Hume and Locke, and of the Methodists. The Christ of westerners was the source of that power, that logic and propulsion. The bucket of a well was reflecting all the vast universe in its water. 'Glory to the bucket,' said the fish. And the pulley only turned faster.

Madhusudhan Dutt, Bengali poet, became Michael Madhusudhan Dutt. He had converted to Christianity. Thus he thought he was worshipping the God of gods. As for Raja Ram Mohan Roy (1772-1883), herald of modern India, he was a Brahmin, well-versed in Sanskrit, Persian, Arabic, and later English. Having read the Bible in that language, he began to study Hebrew and Greek to read the Old and New Testaments in the original. In Persian (the official language of the time), he wrote a life of Jesus, with a preface in Arabic. He also translated the texts of the Upanishads in Bengali, and later in English. 'Humanist' reform was meeting with tradition. Thus, was created the Brahmo Samaj. In the Brahmo Samaj, the Absolute of the Upanishads seems to confirm the God of the Christians: it is no longer necessary to become a Christian to discover God, but the God of the Christians reveals man to us, universal man. Let us love man then. Rites and castes are now hindrances to spiritual life. Misery is not a question of caste, but of ignorance. The wife who burnt herself on her husband's pyre is no longer a symbol of divinity, but a poor victim. Let us tear up orthodox Hinduism. Glory to Brahman! Glory to universal man!

Tagore was born in the Palace of Jorasanko. 'It was an imposing structure, the frames of which seemed to stretch according to their fancy, with vast verandas, immense rooms distributed around the entry, and a series of corridors, staircases, and dark rooms where the sun never penetrated, causing our quavering childhood fears . . .

On the roofs ran a terrace (. . .) so large that two tennis courts could fit and was the center of our life.'

Rathindranath Tagore

In this palace of the new British town, the Tagores ruled over the seasons of steamboats. Tagore's brother himself bought a steamboat to compete with the British and fight for national independence. He naturally went bankrupt. Though Tagore's father was one of the leaders of this reformist movement, Brahmo Samaj, Tagore was too much of a poet to be a puritan. He had some of the inner eye of Leonardo, cosmic spirit of Goethe, revolutionary fire of Victor Hugo, and universalism of Tolstoi. Having inherited all this tradition (they were declaiming Victor Hugo in French in Calcutta; Tagore read Goethe in German), Tagore tapped into the Upanishads, mystical tradition of Bengal, and spoke to God of man. Thus, inspired by the Old Testament, his 'Fruit Gathering' reminds us of Solomon's *Song of Songs*:

The joy ran from all the world to build my body.
The lights of the skies kissed and kissed her till she woke.
Flowers of hurrying summers sighed in her breath and
voices of winds and
water sang in her movements.
The passion of the tide of colours in the clouds and in
forests flowed into her life, and the music of all things
caressed her limbs into shape.

She is my bride—she has lighted her lamp in my house.

Fruit Gathering LXXII
Translation by Raja Rao and Mireille Chapelle

And he sings the glory of woman:

O woman, you are not merely the handiwork of God, but
also of men;
these are ever endowing you with beauty from their
hearts . . .
The desire of men's hearts has shed its glory over your
youth.
You are one half woman and one half dream.

The Gardener LIX
Translation by Raja Rao and Mireille Chapelle

But in the mystical transposition, woman becomes a child, and the beloved, King. Amal, the child, awaits a letter from the King, for why would the King's servants have planted his flags and postal office in front of Amal's house? Men pass by, playful children, women, roadmenders, dervishes. Amal will receive a letter from the King, for Amal cannot leave his home. He is ill. When he sees the mountains rise and merge into space, the horizon shine with the setting sun, Amal thinks that one day he will become the King's courier and deliver the King's letter to the whole world. But the King himself comes to Amal to bring him the message.

Tagore's God is a horizonal god, a god of the highways, an eye-level god. The couriers on the road move forever and

ever; the courier of the King knocks at the door and says:
'Here is, child, a letter from the King'. Rain falls, children
play when the sun rises, but he, the courier, makes his way.
He sings, the message bearer, but doesn't fly, doesn't ascend to
heaven—does not become air or ether, does not dissolve in it.
He is not Krishna, driver of the chariot who, in the midst of
the battle with two armies lined up face to face, says to Arjuna,
the man: 'Knowing the Self, established in the Truth, fight,
therefore, for there is neither killer nor killed.'

There lies the contradiction between the Bhagavad Gita
and the *Gitanjali* of Rabindranath Tagore. Tagore's world is
vast, green, and peaceful, like India in his famous hymn which
became our national anthem:

> Thou art the ruler of the minds of all people,
> Dispenser of India's destiny.
> Thy name rouses the hearts of the Panjaub, Sind,
> Gujarat . . .
> It echoes in the hills of the Vindhyas and Himalayas,
> Mingles in the music of the Jamuna and Ganges,
> And is chanted by the waves of the Indian Sea. . . .

Translation by Raja Rao and Mireille Chapelle

Tagore rises as one of India's certainties, a river, an ancient
capital remained alive, prince of renowned lineage, poet, a
great poet as lived in the times of the Rig-Vedas. He reminds
us of the Vedic bard Vishvamitra in his lyricism and majesty.
He might have been a host in the middle of a peaceful and
luxuriant forest, the master teaching his pupils in the time of
the Upanishads. He might have been a disciple of the great

fourth-century poet Kalidasa, but not of the cynical fifth-century Bhartrihari. He could have been a Moghul poet who came secretly, as did Emperor Akbar, according to tradition, to hear the mystical Queen Mirabai. But Mirabai had Krishna as her god. Tagore only has God, and the God of the poet is a singer.

Tagore founded his school, Santiniketan, a universal school—among the mango trees, under the branches of the pipal trees, tall, venerated and adored—so that man may be brother to men.

Some came from Tokyo, Texas, and even Paris, to hear Tagore sing universal man. He wrote songs and hymns, composed thousands and thousands of them for man, which Hindus still sing today on the roads of India.

> Come, Poet of the people,
> Song of Songs of the mystical man,
> Come, Poet of the new age,
> Bring men's hearts near
> To my distant heart
> So that I may know them through Thee. I salute Thee.

> Translation by Raja Rao and Mireille Chapelle

And then arrived Gandhi.

Gandhi was less interested in man than Truth. Isn't his autobiography titled *The Story of My Experiments with Truth*? In his eyes, in the beginning, God is Truth so we may *finally* dissolve into Truth. Misery, slavery, the suffering of women, disease and death are fatalities that only the search for Truth can cure. Universal man for Gandhi, is the pilgrim of Truth—

*Satyagrahi.* Love, even of others, of a Hindu for an Englishman, of a Hindu for the whole of humanity, can only arise from the discovery of Truth. For Truth takes care of everything. Gandhi before Tagore is a little like Saint Francis before the Pope. Tagore found India too small, too proud for universal man. At the highest of nationalistic times in the world, Tagore was an internationalist. Whereas for Gandhi, every being holds the universe within. To free oneself from personal obstacles, is to make oneself accessible to God—therefore to all His creation. This is how Gandhi returns to the Upanishads.

Tagore, prince and poet, wanted to enjoy the varied colours of the earth, drink from all its sources and know all its possibilities. Darling child of the nineteenth century, he travelled the world from Japan to England; and between England and India, visited many countries, even Russia. The earth is round and round also is Tagore's love, universal love. 'I am surprised,' he wrote from Stockholm in 1921, 'by the large celebrations made in my honour in all these countries. I have often questioned the reason why. I was told that I love humanity. I hope it is really true; and in all my writings, my love for man has found expression and touched men's hearts beyond all barriers.'

There is a very beautiful story in the Indian tradition: One day, a peasant who had just come out of his home found it impossible to walk barefoot, so burning was the ground. Thus, he returned home, climbed to the attic, and discovered a roll of leather with which he covered the ground in front of his house. He then bought other rolls of leather, and more and more rolls to cover the path that led to the village, then rolls that led to the provincial capital, and finally rolls that even led to the royal capital.

The ox hauling them suddenly began to laugh. 'Why are you laughing?' asked the peasant. 'I am able to go all the way to the King's capital without burning my feet.' 'Master of the house,' said the ox, 'instead of creating this gigantic work which will require many a life to complete, if only you carried a little of this leather to the cobbler's so he could make you a pair of sandals, like you shoe my hooves; with these sandals, you could go from villages to provincial towns, and even to the royal capital. But if you prefer to cover the whole earth . . .'

The peasant understood; he went immediately to the cobbler shop and ordered himself a pair of sandals.

Epic novelist, magician of rhythm, friend of astonishing assonances and languishing alliterations, master of imagery, emotional processes and intellectual celebrations, Tagore is also a painter of abstract forms, who at the age of sixty abandoned the realm of the verb for colours and forms. 'It's lines that possess me now,' he would say. 'I am incapable of ridding myself of them. They reveal themselves to me in completely new possibilities. There will be no end to this mystery.'

Further, Tagore is the educator who gave youth a new style—the student of Santiniketan elegantly draped in his robes, a sitar resonating on his shoulder. There is also Tagore the actor, one of the greatest in modern India; and Tagore the musician, who changed the history of Indian music by its original synthesis with European music: daily, the Radio plays songs from the Rabindra Sangeet—Rabindranath's music. And there is Tagore, the politician, who summoned the British to subscribe to their commitments, chastised imperialists everywhere; Tagore, Mussolini's guest, Stalin's guest, Gandhi's friend. Tagore finally, master agronomist, who experimented on fertilizers with new principles, as he had done with metrics.

Tagore, Renaissance figure, is not a man of our time. It is our good fortune that he was a contemporary. Since Leonardo of Florence, there has been no figure as prestigious and universal as this *Gangaputra,* this son of the Ganges.

# 9

# Books Which Have Influenced Me

I am obsessed with Sanskrit.

In recent years I have been exalted by and fascinated with Malayalam, which is over eighty percent Sanskrit. Naturally, my own mother tongue, Kannada, touches elemental chords in me. French seems to me a language for the aristocracy of the spirit. Italian is a language of golden humanity, the *dolce verbe toscane*. English is of Shakespeare. Hindi has the innocence, the young, rolling cadence of the Ganga at Hardwar. Urdu has the spirit of Ghalib.

Lord, what a lot of tongues, and a lot of books to read! If you choose Bossuet's, you might be reminded of the royal precision of Bhartrihari; if reading Leopardi, you might suddenly slip down and find yourself on the ghats of Varanasi with Kabir weaving depth into his poetry. Though Leopardi's sorrow seems too reasonable, too human beside Kabir's magnanimity and dedication.

The *Vachanakaras,* of the thirteenth and fourteenth centuries, in Kannada, reminded me of Baudelaire, but without his negative excitement for vice. But if vice were white, you would find it in Damodaragupta, who after invoking Shiva's blessings wrote of the bawds of Varanasi in robust Sanskrit. La Rochefoucauld seems inhibited (remember, he wore garters and a wig and must have smelt bad despite his perfumes) side by side with the *Hitopadesha*.

I have read Dante's *Paradiso* in Varanasi and found it familiar. I have read Tulsidas in Tuscany—sitting by Dante's Arno in Florence—and found him surprisingly contemporary. The Arno is a younger river than the Saraju. If you looked up and saw the San Miniato, the battlements of Michelangelo, running down in young leaps of turreted silences—as if time were a substance one could catch and keep, *Fiorenza dentro dalla cerchia antica*—you might see Sri Rama Himself, with Vasishta and Lakshmana, emerging from behind them. The sun of Tuscany seems oft-times the light of Ayodhya.

The Seine, one feels, understands Shankara as no other river in Europe could, while having a premonition of the verbal alchemy of wisdom and the Word. *Vak-aksara*, etc., etc . . . I have often recited Kalidasa to the Seine, and she seemed to remember him. After all, books, though made out of words, are ultimately understood where no words are. That being so, what books shall I say have influenced me?

Those that have done so the most are perhaps the books I have never read, at least never fully. The one that has influenced me above all, though, as it has every Indian, is the *Ramayana*. What could be more glorious, more sacred, more fantastic than this book of books. It reveals every beauty and treachery of our tragi-comic existence, the absurd, inhuman, gentle, devout, noble, and cruel, yet not altogether felt of this world. No other book better enlightens, for our terror and joy, and final wisdom, than the Ramayana. Valmiki's

Ramayana, of course. It is the book that some widow seated in a dim room by the ghats in Varanasi or Srirangam might, by a patch of kerosene light, be reading—trying to cover her shaven head with the falling folds of an ochre sari while not understanding why Rama was so harsh to Sita. Weeping with Sita but still worshiping Sri Rama and exulting in the devotion of Hanuman to his Supreme Lord.

It is the Ramayana that has filled my imagination over the years, coming to me at every critical point in my life to interpret and to help. After all, which masculine figure in all literature could be more admirable than Lakshmana, unless it be Bhishma? But Bhishma I discovered much later, though it was he made me understand India and the Indian experience. One who does not understand Bhishma and through Bhishma's words Sri Krishna himself, will never *know* India.

एह्योहि फुल्लाम्बुजपत्रनेत्र नमोस्तु ते माधव चक्रपाणे ।
प्रसह्य मां पातय लोकनाथ रथोत्तमात्सर्वशरण्य सङ्ख्ये ॥
त्वया हतस्यपि ममाद्य कृष्ण श्रेयः परस्मिन्निह चैव लोके ।
सम्भावितोस्म्यन्धकवृष्णिनाथ लोकैस्त्रिभिर्वीर तवाभियानात् ॥
—भीष्मपर्व

ehyehi phullāmbujapatranetra namostu te mādhava
cakrapāṇe ।
prasahya māṃ pataya lokanātha rathottamatsarvaśaraṇya
saṅkhye ॥
tvayā hatasyapi mamādya kṛṣṇa śreyaḥ parasminniha caiva
loke ।
sambhāvitosmyandhakavṛṣṇinātha lokaistribhirvīra
tavābhiyānāt ॥
—Bhīṣmaparva

After the Ramayana and the Mahabharata, neither of which I have read in full, the book that has affected me most is the *Brihatstotraratnakara*. The copy I possess is so crabbed and torn that its pages seem to hide in many places around me wherever I go. This anthology contains some of the most beautiful poetry in Sanskrit, the language I know so poorly but intuit so deeply, and generates waves of holiness. In its pages live Shankara, Valmiki, and Kalidasa, even Jaganatha Bhatta.

Buddhist texts have also stirred me, but I have read them mostly in English or French translations. I am drawn to their poetry and rich humanity.

> As when it rains the scrubs
> and grasses,
> The bushes and the smaller
> plants,
> The trees and also the great
> woods
> Are all made splendid in the ten
> regions;
> So the nature of Dharma exists
> for the wheel of the world,
> And it refreshes by this Dharma
> the entire world.
> And then refreshed, just like the plants,
> The world will burst forth into
> blossoms.
>
> Translation by Ed Conze

But, there being something of the Kshatriya in me, I always go back to the Ramayana and the Mahabharata.

भारतानां महज्जन्म महाभारतमुच्यते ।
भरताद्धारती कीर्तिर्येनेदं भारतं कुलम् ॥
—आदिपर्व

*bhāratānāṃ mahajjanma mahābhāratamucyate |*
*bharatādbhāratī kīrtiryenedaṃ bhārataṃ kulam ॥*

—Ādiparva

In Kannada, the *Vachanakaras*, the *Kanakadasa,* and the *Purandaradasa* have affected me so profoundly that they have changed my style of writing. Shakespeare, too, is fundamental to me, *Hamlet* first and foremost, then *King Lear*, and finally *The Tempest*. He is almost an Indian of my India. And no man could have read Plato without feeling that here was a companion of all pilgrimages.

Man's roots are many, but they all lead to his centre. He is like our *aswatta* tree, the morning sun playing on its young, hypostatic leaves, its ancient, severe trunk sunk into the wood of the sacred platform and surrounded with worshipful *naga* stones. Below it runs a river. Many a pilgrim will adorn and make circumambulations of this aswatta tree.

But where's the god, you ask, the temple? The tree is the temple, too old to be named; going round and round it, you feel holy. The leaves celebrate and shine in the sun.

The books I have read, like the ghats I have trod, are just the steps down to the river. Lord, what holiness there be on this earth!

त्रिभुवनजननी व्यापिनी ज्ञानगङ्गा ॥
—काशीपञ्चकम्

*tribhuvanajananī vyāpinī jñānagaṅgā* ‖

—*Kāśīpañcakam*

The books that have influenced me in no cognizable manner are those I loved as a young man. First was Dostoevski and his *The Brothers Karamazov*, which I discovered, while still a student, in a second-hand bookshop off the Boulevard St. Michel in Paris. Since it was raining, I slid the book under my overcoat, and returning to my damp, unfamiliar room, read page after page as if the story had all happened around and to me.

The year before, I had read, in that extraordinarily poetical un-French French of his, Romain Rolland's *Jean Christophe*. It left a deep intellectual mark on me. When younger still, Mazzini's *Duties of Man* greatly impressed me. But the book back then that would prove of lasting influence on my life was Mahatma Gandhi's *My Experiments with the Truth*. I read it at the Nizam College reading room as the text came out, week after week, in the journal *Young India*.

In my more mature years, two authors, both French, and incidentally, friends of one another, have influenced me: Paul Valery and Andre Gide. Valery was not only one of the major poets of our century, if not its greatest, but also a prose writer of classical integrity. His critical essays, and especially his short novel *Monsieur Teste*, sharpened my intellectual processes, and made learning the rigours of literary discipline an exhilarating task. André Gide, meanwhile, outshone Valéry in his humanity and precise sense of the play of ethics and poetic sensibility. His *Porte Etroite*, with its anguished fervour and accomplished simplicity of style, is a minor masterpiece.

During World War II, I travelled a great deal in India, with the passion and devotion of a pilgrim. During all those years, three authors accompanied me: Rainer Maria Rilke and his *Duino Elegies* (in Stephen Spender and Lieshman's excellent translation), along with a rich treasury of his letters to friends; W. B. Yeats and his autobiography, which I consider one of the greatest books in the English tongue; and Franz Kafka—who has not been influenced by him? His *The Castle* and *The Trial* are among the basic tales of contemporary mythology.

Nor should I forget to mention Gorki and his singularly moving book of the human condition, *Mother.* Also *Fontamara,* by Ignazio Salone, which combines folklore and politics, raising each to a new level of poetical experience. But the master of them all is Walt Whitman, whose *Leaves of Grass* will be read with intimacy and awe as long as man seeks to praise the intangible present.

The only *living* writer who has influenced me is André Malraux. Not merely his novels, important as they are, but his aesthetic essays that have a metaphysical acuity and importance that will outlast most of what has appeared in our times.

Then there is Ananda Coomaraswamy. No sensitive Indian could have read his books, any of his books, without realizing that one had discovered an India that he'd felt, but never been able to name. For as Coomaraswamy expressed—whether it be through Dante or Shakespeare, St. Thomas Aquinas or Nietzsche—you come back to the Upanishads and the Vedanta, reasoning that wheresoever you go, you will always return to the Himalayas. And whatever the rivers that flow, the waters are of the Gangotri.

# Part II

# Vac, the Word

# 10

# The Fable Goes Round

Scholars often have a way of making simple things complicated and complicated things seem so simple that it all looks outrageous fun. For example, Weber and Benfey were not sure if the fable and the German *marchen* (which the Grimm brothers used a great deal) were of Greek or Indian origin, as the scholars Wagener and Rhys Davids believed.

In fact, we simply do not know where fables began, Greece or India, and ultimately, does it matter much? The truth is fables have given delight to millions of people all over the world and continue to do so unto this very day. Or as the good La Fontaine said of the fable:

> *Une ample Comédie, aux cent actes divers,*
> *Et dont la scène est l'Univers*

Yet the history of the fable looks like a fable itself, dealing as it does with wolf and lion, jackal and tiger, tortoise and mouse— these starting where, who starting which, what coming from where, who translating what, and when? Whether in its westward travel the jackal of India became the wolf—not so clever an animal as the jackal, you will agree—doesn't matter; the story probably came from India. Or why not it be the fox of Aesop—also not so clever—for one was not after all telling a psychological tale but inventing a fable. Finally, the differences between the serious scholars were somewhat reduced by suggesting it was perhaps neither Greece nor India, but a product of lands lying between those two countries.

Then the quarrel went a step further and moved the story back in history, the scholars scratching their long ears and saying, 'Why not Egypt?' The scholar Hertzel made an even bigger leap, surmising there must have been an archetypal basis for *all* the stories, and called it 'T'—from which all the jackals, wolves, geese, tortoises, tigers, and so forth flowed.

Nor should we forget our humble servant, the ass. In fact, La Fontaine was right: the trouble started not with the tiger or the jackal but with the unfortunate donkey. As he says:

À *ces mots on cria haro sur le baudet.*

The poor braying ass, indeed, was known even to Plato—he speaks of it in the *Cratylus*.

What we cannot say for sure is whether the fabled owner of this lowly animal was a washerman or a merchant; the caste changes with time and geography. Originally, he is just a washerman, one of those still known in India as a *dhobi,* who makes these beasts of burden carry soiled clothes.

One day, this washer of clothes, finding a tiger dead in the jungle, cleaned the skin and brought it home. The clothes-laundering business not yielding enough for either man or beast, his wretched donkey was very lean and shaky. Trying to ease the poor creature's misery, he wrapped him in the tiger skin and turned him loose at night in his neighbours' wheat fields to graze. When this 'tiger' was spotted people fled in fear; it was dark, you understand, and they could not see clearly. When day came, the beast would resume carrying clothes to the river. He grew fat.

One night, however, the donkey smelt the female of his species, started braying, and she gave a becoming answer. One villager, hearing this and realizing the deception, took cudgel and knife and cut the outed impostor to bits.

As the donkey's tale wandered in time downward, and in space westward, it would seem (unless it traveled eastward and upward, which is after all, according to Benfey and Weber, only a question of reversing the process) that the animal's noble, nocturnal disguise changed. As did the caste of its owner. The donkey became a lion and the washerman a merchant according to the Buddha, who telling one of his birth stories ended with the remark:

> This is not a lion's roar,
> Nor a tiger's, nor a panther's.
> Dressed in a lion's skin
> 'Tis a wretched ass that roars.

Two thousand years later, La Fontaine said almost the same thing when he wrote:

> *De la peau du lion l'âne s'étant vêtu*
> *Était craint partout à la ronde,*
> *Et bien qu' animal sans vertu*
> *Il faisait trembler tout le monde.*

In the quarrel between scholars, La Fontaine definitely takes sides. In the foreword to his collection of tales, he says, '*Seulement je dirai, par reconnaissance, que j'en dois la plus grande partie à Pilpay, sage indien. Son livre a* été *traduit en toutes les langues.*' He talks of the girl who goes with the milk pot on her head—'*Perrette, sur sa* tête, *ayant un Pot au lait Bien posé sur un coussinet*'—which is nothing else than that other fable of the unfortunate Brahmin, who, with his jar of barley meal, which was gathered from days of alms-begging and was hanging on the wall bedside him, dreams one night of a lovely future wife.

In the dream they have a son named Moon Lord. When the father sees the child wandering unattended near the horses (for by then he would have horses and stables), afraid lest the child be trampled, he pulls him to safety. Still in his dream, he runs to his negligent wife and gives her a rollicking kick. Unfortunately, this results in him shattering his very *real* jar of barley meal, the source of his imagined future riches, scattering the meal all about the floor.

We also have La Fontaine's tale of the tortoise on its way to see the republics of America, carried along by biting onto a stick supported between two flying geese. When people mocked at him from below, he answered back—and fell.

The Indian tortoise, too, falls, but these geese are not winging him to enchanting destinations. In this tale, there being a twelve-year drought upon the land, the geese take a stick of wood in their beaks and ferry him to a surviving pool of water. Again, hanging by his beak, a tortoise begins his aerial adventure. In the stories of the *Panchatantra,* the tortoise made many similar but more successful voyages, saw many epochs and lands, and was carried by many geese.

Actually, the *Panchatantra* is nonexistent in its original form, though it must have been written by the mythical Vidyapathi (Lord of Learning), who through his travels became, to La Fontaine, the Indian sage Pilpay. At first, the book was only in Sanskrit, until Khosrow Anushirvan, King of Iran in the years 531-579, hearing of its wise and famous fables, sent his doctor, Barzouey, to find this 'treasury of wisdom'. Barzouey wrote a Pahlavi version, which Abdullah Ibn al-Muqaffa, a Persian converted to Islam, translated into beautiful Arabic in the year 750.

There was also a Syriac rendition of the *Panchatantra* by Bud, and a second, from the Arabic to Syriac, three centuries later. Meanwhile, the Arabic version travelled and was given a Greek translation by Simon Seth, a Jew. In 1100, John of Capua transformed a Hebrew text of Rabbi Joel's into Latin, which the Duke of Württemberg, Eberhard the 1st, translated into German in 1470, calling it *Beispiele der Weisen Geschlecht zu Geschlecht*. This was later rendered into Danish, Icelandic, and Dutch. Meanwhile, Joan of Navarre, the Castilian wife of King Phillip IV of France (1285-1384), had her doctor, Raymond de Béziers, translate the collection into her native tongue.

Anton Doni created an Italian version from which Sir Thomas North, in 1570, made his famed English translation, calling it *The Morall Philosophie of Doni*. La Fontaine's *The Apollogues de Bidpai* didn't appear until 1644, but he seems to have used the Latin text of the *Panchatantra;* in it, the two jackal brothers in the retinue of the lion king, *Calila et Dinna,* are the Latinized names of Karataka and Damanaka. La Fontaine's Latin text coming from the Greek of Simon Seth. He had heard of these stories from his friend, the renowned traveller Francois Bernier.

By now, the Portuguese Alfonso de Albuquerque had sailed to India, followed by the French, then the English. There he attended the court of the Great Moghul, Akbar, who himself had asked his vizier, Abul Fazl, to have the *Panchatantra* translated from Sanskrit into Arabic. With all this foreign influence came Indian schools that taught children the marvels of the Western world, eager students encountering many interesting fables, stories, and poems in their English classes. When they read, for instance, the Welsh folktale of Prince Llywelyn's hound, Gelert, they delighted at this wonderful story of the faithful dog that protected the master's child. Then, in their Sanskrit classes, from the *Panchatantra* they discovered the dog had turned mongoose, protecting the child of the good Brahmin from the serpent. Eventually, Narayana Balkrishna Godpole, a schoolmaster at Agmednagar, would return all these European fables to Sanskrit, and thus the fable ended as a fable of the fable.

There's an old Indian adage which says that you become what you contemplate. The story of some of these fable-makers is often like a fable itself. Alfred Williams of South Marston, near Swindon, England, was a poor workman at the forge. He also cultivated his little bit of land, and when he had time, he and his devoted wife built a cottage there, stone by stone. In between working at the forge and on the cottage, Williams studied books on Latin and Greek. Then came the Great War of 1914, and he volunteered, ending up in India. While he was not soldiering, he learnt Sanskrit. Coming back after the war to wife and home, he crafted the *Panchatantra*, this most translated of books but for the Bible, into beautiful English prose. But just as the book was at the press, the poor man died. Six weeks later, stricken with grief, his wife followed him.

Fables in sooth are not what they appear,
Our moralists are mice and such small deer.
We yawn at sermons, but we gladly turn
To moral tales, and so amused, we learn.

\* \* \*

## Thoughts From an Essay Accompanying 'The Fable Goes Round'

If culprits there be who plagiarized these tales, they might be found among the silk, spice, and muslin merchants from various countries of Asia who gathered in Samarkand. From there they travelled to Asia Minor, some to North Africa and Spain, others through Greece and Gaul. Whether or not their friends and friends of friends had met in Frankfort or Aix La Chappelle or anywhere, they told the same story of Karataka and Damanaka, with, of course, variations. And must have wondered whence the fable came.

In selling their silk to the Western aristocracy (Rome bought so much muslin that a law had to be passed to discourage its use), the merchants shared their tales with their refined women customers, and these yet again with their children. When the children grew up and started wandering the globe as soldiers or administrators, they told the stories at parties round their drinks. Thus was the fable spread all over the known world.

Later, some medieval scholar, in trying to find the texts' Arabic and Syriac origins, translated them into Latin, which became famous as the works of La Fontaine's Pilpay. So that today, when a French child begins to sing '*Autrefois le Rat de ville'*, who can say which Indian, Greek, or Chinese antecedent created this lovely fable?

The reason for the symbolic use of animals in fables is quite simple. Animals even today live in intimacy with man, and one makes use in one's fiction of what is most familiar. If some Indian courtier wants to say something nasty about his colleague, he has but to declare, 'As the Bull said to the Jackal . . .' And those who understood, understood.

Montesquieu invented imaginary Persians in his satirical novel, *The Persians*. Whether Persians or animals, they are used to bring home a truth. So as the jackal, which had no tail, convinced other jackals of the virtue of having no tail, so did the minister out of favour trick other ministers into quitting their jobs so he could have his again. Thus, the prince was taught this cut-your-brother's-tail psychology, so that when he became king he could keep his state in order.

Indian or Greek, the fables differed little in their cleverness. Boccaccio later amused his listeners with tales of widows and lovers, while Chaucer entertained a whole century of English pilgrims. The story of a faithful Hindu lover suffering tribulations became *Tristan and Isolde*, medieval storytellers making it into one of the West's great tragedies.

Wagner with his music made whole generations weep. Who in Bayreuth, Germany, would have guessed he was being moved by a Hindu wife from some long-ago millennium? Similarly, what peasant in French Béarn would realize that the in-turned circle around a broken cross hanging on his wall, supposed to bring him good fortune, is also the sign of the *svastika* on the wall of a Hindu? Or which shepherd from the Dauphiné Alps knows that *sapin*, the pine, as his Larousse dictionary would tell him, comes from the Sanskrit *sapa*? And

what Italian hotel porter jangling his *chiavi*, his keys, would
know that his colleague in the Taj Mahal Hotel in Bombay
calls them *chiavi*, too?

A united world was not created yesterday—it has always
existed. Thought has always flown from country to country,
and back again to its country of origin. People did not live
in nations, they lived in the world. The world, flat or round,
was one, and belonged to all. In ancient times, if you wanted
to trade in silk, you joined a caravan, sharing stories at every
caravanserai. Then, returning to the banks of the Rhone or
the Rhine, you'd be greeted with the same story. Everyone
had a good laugh over this.

We may laugh, too, and ask why complicate matters
by wondering if the Greeks borrowed from the Indians or
the Indians from the Greeks? It is like pondering whether
Shakespeare wrote the plays and sonnets we have come to
know as his. The fact remains, we still read Shakespeare. And
he is universal.

# 11

# The Climate of Indian Literature Today

The Calcutta trams seem voluble. They love to speak in one long, twangy tongue. The Bengali language, the Provençal of the East, has a lilt and a lug that seem to sparkle corners, and rush through crowded streets proclaiming its many-rhythmed accommodation to both song and silence. The cows that lie by the tram lines or on the lawns of the *maidan* have a ruminant rhythm that appears to make poetry as simple as a munch of grass on the autumnal bend of the round evenings. 'Evening, her eyes downcast, slowly follows the trail of day . . .'

The Calcutta poets have a declamation that is at once ancient and international. 'The whole world, however wide, was but homeland extended,' said Tagore. Though Bengali speech has much Sanskrit and a secret preference for Mallarméan enigma, '*Tout orgeuil fume-t-il du soir*'.

Rilke also seems to dream in Bengali, talking of pyramids and the Champs-Élysées. The fact of the matter is that poetry is as natural to the Bengali as water. The Ganges has made Bengal one of the richest harvest lands in the country, with its many gilded waterways and its estuary, the Ganga-Sagar, the

Ganges-ocean. The Padma is what the Ganges calls herself in Bengal, a river that Tagore so dearly sang about. 'How often have I thought, sitting on thy bank, that in some afterlife I return to this earth and row a boat on thy swift stream . . . that some deep consciousness will wake.'

The songs of Tagore have shaped even the trees of Bengal, the new, agile speech of the Bengali makes magic with his eyes. The Bengali is so truly a poet that out of the Gangetic clay he makes women into little village divinities. When the monsoon pours, the potters shape them into goddesses which one buys in the bazaars, takes home, and worships with garlands, incense and sweetmeats, milk and water. And, of course, love.

Hence Calcutta, which means the waterside of the goddess Kali. The poet ever and always worships his love in Bengali.

> Urgent, uncertain, ruthless, full of violence,
> The water foamed and spread and disappeared
> Into the final silence of the Fates
> When I left my love in the hand of God.
> Buddhadeva Bose

All poetry of love . . . was it not first sung in Bengali speech? Or should one call it Provençal? Does it matter? The modern Calcutta poet with his sip of whiskey or vermouth, his elaborate quotations from Verlaine or Goethe, seems imbued with hunger, anger, despair—and dialectics.

> The earthworm wanted to know the earth.
> Its canals and fields in holes and clefts
> It sought to know the utmost reaches of the earth.

The earthworm wanted to know the earth.
Neither in mud nor in slush,
Neither by crawling nor rolling,
Did it find the secret of the earth.
It then sought the answer in its body's sap.

At last the earthworm died.
It died ignorant of the drama of the earth.

                              Unknown

The Bengali, like the Italian, loves nomenclature. And like the Italian marble that made the architecture of Petrarch, the Bengali boatmen's prayers have made Bengali verse.

We are people of the land of rivers.
Its heart is wide open to us.
And to it we return.

                              Humayun Kabir

The boats, like ancient Egyptian watercraft, have fisheyes, which is to say, all smoothness, shine, and perenniality. The volubility of Bengal, therefore, breaks out into many-vowelled song. The great eighth-century Sanskrit critic Dandin, however, said that the Bengali style is that of *akshara adambara*, a concatenation of sound-clangings. Though in time the consonants smoothed into a flashing flow. Thus, the trams run on.

In April 1942, far in the south, amidst the coconut gardens of Kerala, a literary gathering was held, the fifth All India Writer's Conference. The twelve (or are there fourteen?) Indian languages were represented, and even the English language was invited thither, with some condescension. This imperial speech seemed to have other accents too, other promises. It was a bastardization of foreign associations, themes, and rhythms, a grammar and idiom cold, both unrelated and confusing. With its dastardly 'ats' and 'ons', the English language could only be treated as a nouveau riche would be among impoverished ancients. In discomfort and pride, it tried to hide itself wheresoever and whensoever it could; there were always vacant corner seats at this many-tongued conference.

There were even the ever-prominent Russians speaking Russian, the Yugoslavs speaking Serbo-Croatian, and a few American professors trying to speak every tongue they could.

The president, a distinguished poet—tall, bearded, once a revolutionary, later a man of the establishment, now a literary revolutionary and an elder—spoke an inaugural speech entitled 'India cannot have a literature except in an Indian language.' Regrettably, he gave the speech in cadenced and highly manipulated English. It was taken by all, however, that he spoke in the chastest of Hindi:

> We are not those who act,
> Nor follow those who follow those who act.
>
> Unless it be said we exposed
> A fresh layer of the raw pain of being human,
> Found a crack in the crushing wall,
> And the shunning light that shot through the
> Crack.
> We gave that light a name.
> Come, my friends, let us give that light name.

And that name, of course, is Hindi, and this its new poetry.

The truth was the southern people, highly sophisticated and Dravidic in their inspiration but rich in Sanskritic traditions, refused to be spoken to in Hindi, a raw latecomer to Indian literature. Although it be the official language of the Republic of India. Hindi was mainly spoken at this conference in soft corners where the northerners held their councils.

The Tamil writers, bold and proud, spoke English as a way of demeaning Hindi literature. They talked, but with evident mischief behind it, of the inadequacies of Tamil performances in drama, the short story, and the novel. We denigrate our writers, they seemed to say, and call them 'sold-at-the-film-booths or to the cent-a-word magazines', because we think you with your new Hindi and northern arrogance (youth always has arrogance) have nothing better to show than we. By calling our colleagues names, they added, we want you to shut up and not taunt us with your languid, self-inflated speech.

The other writers, however, speaking a less elegant English, made long-winded declamations about the glory of Oriya or Assamese achievements (the Nobel Prize had a claimant in every language of India), and the Bengali attendees rounded it all into bucolic English prose.

Speaking of the beauty of the Himalayas, Kalidasa said, 'Even the gods will require aeons to describe it. Oh, Kerala, when I contemplate thy different moods, I get bewildered and feel like a great and ancient poet.' Vowels were never mouthed with better rhythm than in this Gangetic shine and flow. The Bengali was at home everywhere, even in English, and his statements had sonority, certainty, and lotus-whiteness. And his language had achieved nationhood. Remember Tagore's Nobel Prize.

Those at the conference who wrote in English mopped their mid-day tears, afraid but unrepentant. Awkward yet convincing, there was a challenge to this. But the tricky North Indian was not going to give up the game easily. They prepared a poetic manifestation to soothen and soften all pride.

The south Indian, however, would still be won over. Their poet was given the first national prize from Calcutta by a Hindi-dominated group, thus making amends for stealing, as it were, the golden peacock. The prize was given for a long mythological poem. Shri G. Sankara Kurup wrote his winning poem in classical Malayalam, a Dravidic speech having more pure Sanskrit words than any other south Indian language. The poem, of course, spoke of love and heroism, despair and dedication.

Those who gave the prize could not read the southern script, nor its tongue. They had sent an Indian scholar sometime earlier to the Nobel Committee in Stockholm to learn how it recognized writers who wrote in diverse languages. Samples, he was told, of the Malayalam original were supplied in good Swedish to the members of the Academy. And the strategy worked.

Hence, our Calcutta sponsors read the poem in acceptable samples and in an English prose translation. Literally overnight, Shri Kurup—a classical southern poet—became a national figure and a millionaire. Rather, a *lakhpathi,* for the prize was worth a *lakh,* one hundred thousand rupees.

The conference prize was announced among the palm groves and factory chimneys of FACT, Fertilizers and Chemicals of Travancore. This was due to the influence and courtesy of our former minister of Oils and Gases, a well-known politician *and* poet. On the morning of the last day, the long-awaited awards procession began.

It was much like the first act of *Sakuntala*, where the king was somewhere a-hunting. The audience could only hear noises, and see a group of girls in traditional dress, hair knotted in forest-maiden fashion, curved, black, conch-like, above their crowns. Their bosoms were full, fresh, and clad in multi-colours, their saris white and hanging from the waist. They processioned toward the guest house, bearing lamps like so many lotuses in their hands.

Then, like a bridegroom, or Sakuntala's King Dushyantha,

> A king of Puru's mighty line
> Chastises shameless churls;
> What insolent is he who baits
> These artless hermit-girls.

Act I

The poet-millionaire, clothed in a simple southern dhoti and a shirt, with a shawl draped over his shoulders, came out in all humility and gratitude to be received by the maidens. They, with garland, flame, and chant, escorted him to the rostrum set in a pandal made of bamboo, coconut leaves, cloth bunting, and photographs. There he gave his acceptance speech in Malayalam, which few of the delegates understood except for the occasional Sanskrit word. We were sure, Kurup having received our first national Nobel Prize, that he was a good and great poet, a *Mahakavi*, one day to be read by future generations in all the Indian languages. Some of us had tears in our eyes, so moving was it all.

The chairman spoke a few words of praise and homage, after which the conference dispersed. The Bombay writers who wrote *haiku* in Marathi, the Kannada writers who penned famous plays of humour and pathos, the Delhi director of our National School of Drama—an Arab by blood, Indian by birth, who had presided over our meetings with distinction and clarity in beautifully modulated English—all went back to their hometowns. Some had taken this unique opportunity to bring their families on pilgrimage. Paper kites, fluttering against the sea wind, hung from coconut trees. What language did *they* speak, one wonders?

\* \* \*

In the royal city of Mysore, there was a seminar on Indian literature organized by one of the ablest of India's literary critics (and a student of F.R. Leavis of Cambridge), an arrogant Anglicist and master of English prose. There, writer after writer proclaimed the virtues of his language—but they all had a sorry story to tell. Names like Gorky and Camus, T.S. Eliot and Yeats were brought up in speeches and discussions. One man, an encyclopaedia of modern Indian learning, spoke for every unrepresented language.

Some speakers had more pride than perspicacity, others more sarcasm than comfort, while others spoke in dithyrambs of an almost obsolete tongue. There was so much confusion and confession, that we looked at each other wondering at the state of literature in India today.

Everyone spoke in English with either reverence toward the past or unconvinced pride or humiliation at the present. After mention of Hemingway and Sartre and the rest, all looked across the valley toward the Hill of the Goddess, desperately seeking a clearer statement for guidance.

On top of the hill, the Maharaja himself had come to worship his family deity. Amidst the sound of temple bells and Sanskrit hymns, everyone longed for some intimation of where Indian literature was both coming from and going to. To inherit Sanskrit and yet be so lost, despite the names of Joyce, Beckett, and D.H. Lawrence on our lips, was a confession that signified grace alone is our only hope—the Guru's grace. It alone enabled Shankara to write such metaphysical poetry as India had never seen. Or Kalidasa, a lowly cowherd, as a gift from the Goddess Kali, able to speak in classical Sanskrit verse.

In other words, Indian literature was looking to the heavens for an answer. Whereas the hungry and angry cry themselves hoarse in verse and prose in the pages of too-forgiving magazines which insist that T.S. Eliot and Sartre did not live in vain. Nor even Baudelaire.

# 12

# The Story Round, Around Kanthapura

*Kanthapura* had a bewildering destiny.

I wrote most of the novel in the thick, high tower of a thirteenth-century castle, the Chateau de Montmaur in the Hautes-Alpes. The castle of Montmaur was the hunting retreat of the dauphins of France. As I sat and wrote, day after day, I felt the snow high behind me though I could not see it from my tower. In the valley beneath meandered a little river, and beyond lay a wall of towering green mountains; the river actually was more a peaceful, white-gurgling stream. The alpine peace, though pure, was set in the midst of turbulent history. It was the time of Hitler in Germany, Mussolini in Italy, and Franco's fierce Spanish Civil War, in which the former collaborated in plying their new machines of destruction.

*Kanthapura* was first published in February of 1938. It had a certain critical success but was not widely read, or so complained Sir Stanley Unwin, my publisher. However, an English literary agent wrote an urgent letter to me asking permission for the translation rights to the novel into Czech. Hitler had just walked into Prague, and the book wasn't wanted for its literary value but its essentially Gandhian motif. Of course, I agreed at once. But I never heard if it was published or not—the translation I mean—for war was soon to spread across Europe.

Fortunately, because of health reasons, by then I was back in India; if I had stayed in Europe, I would probably not be writing this today. I had contact with anti-fascist groups from all over Europe—and a vegetarian and Gandhian had no place under Marshal Pétain. I later heard the French police had orders to arrest me.

Before I left Menton with friends for India in July 1939, a Dutch novelist, A.M. de Jong, whom I had met earlier, asked me for the translation rights of the book, and I gave them. The ominous cloud of war was hanging over Europe, and I understood de Jong's intentions. Indeed, while I was with Gandhiji in Sevagram, Hitler invaded Holland.

All of Europe was soon lost to Hitler, but India under the British wasn't free, either. When peace finally came to both, Achut Patwardhan, the leader of the Gandhian Uprising from 1942–1945, was going to Holland for an eye operation. I asked him to try and contact de Jong. Achut telephoned de Jong's home and learned from the writer's son that his father had been shot by the Nazis. Though I have never been able to verify the story, I've been told the Dutch novelist was arrested while translating *Kanthapura*.

After the war, the world began to show great interest in India, especially in Gandhism. A Swedish publisher who was connected with various left-wing organizations had also brought out an edition of *Kanthapura*. That the book was backed by the leftist press seemed only natural. Then came a Spanish edition from Barcelona, still under the terror of

Franco, and even more significantly one from a Hungary under the tyranny of Communist rule.

Thus was the magic of Gandhi—the Pied Piper of nonviolence and love for one's fellow man—drawn to wheresoever it was needed. It is all part of the Gandhi Purana. I will never forget Gandhiji begging the British government for permission to talk to Hitler, and later pleading with the allies to let him meet with Hirohito of Japan. But Churchill would have none of this; to him, Gandhiji was the 'naked fakir'.

Who knows what effect the Gandhi Purana might have had if Churchill had accepted his challenge? History is full of miracles; remember Ashoka of India, and Saint Louis IX of France. Truth is always superior to the sword—something India herself has to relearn.

# 13

# Why Do You Write?

I write. I cannot not write. Yet, he who writes does not know *that* which writes. So, does one write? If so, who? What writes?

Why write? Two birds, says the Ramayana, our oldest epic, were making love when a hunter killed the male bird. The cry of the widowed bird, reads the text, created the rhythm of the poem. The hero Prince Rama freed his wife Sita, abducted and imprisoned by the monster Ravana, King of Ceylon. Monkeys and bears helped in freeing Sita, seated in sorrow under the asoka tree.

Trees decay, birds cry, man suffers. One writes because of one's compassion for all creatures. *Sokah slokatvam agatah,* 'from sorrow arrives verse'. Thus, *sahitya*—literature—from *sahita*, togetherness.

Why publish? That others may hear the cry of the fallen bird's mate, lost in her sorrow. Uncovering vocables is a noetic exercise. The precise word arises of love, that is, pure intelligence. That is why in Sanskrit, the word *kavi* means the poet—and the sage.

# 14

# Two Proposals

## In Search of Reality: Cosmology, Poetry, Linguistics

By the late nineteenth century, reality was being sought in the details of physical events and everyday life. The sciences were to be exact. Continued improvements in the mechanisms and techniques of observation were to bring deepened insights into the objects of scientific investigation.

Writers, too, began to concentrate on the details of daily existence; Zola, for one, described events punctiliously. To penetrate more deeply into reality, Hauptmann used a dialect scarcely intelligible to anyone outside Silesia in portraying the problems of its weavers. Language was to be plain, stripped of its metaphors and personal idiosyncrasies. Scientists were to write in the passive, and without attribution, relating their conclusions without indicating the role of the inconsequential author. Reality was to be found in facts, posited starkly by both scientist and poet.

The quantum theory set science on a new course. Suddenly, the most minute observations of the most strictly mechanical particles were not objective; instead, the observer affected them by his observations. Reality could no longer be achieved by means of microscope, telescope, or other mechanisms, however powerful.

In quantum theory, the interposition of the individual, no matter how rigorous the scientific procedures, affects the event or process witnessed. The observer is preeminent, crucial in disclosing reality; there is no objective observation. In accordance with his role, the conceptions of causality and time have been modified. Evolution takes place by quantum leaps, not straight lines.

In quantum theory, insights into reality may be available to individuals making observations which do not require mechanical aids. Such individuals have long been recognized, some as poets, some as seers. In the Rig Veda, as is well known, *kavi* is both poet and seer. Through them, the poetic word reveals the unexpected but inevitable, as does the new physics. Through the poetic word, the common world is transcended into reality.

Yet, both scientist and poet are subject to the limitation of human language. Each seeks to escape its bonds—the scientist through an abbreviated language known as mathematics, the poet through an individualized but impersonal language. These efforts at more precise communication, however, have their limits. While mathematics is restricted to quantitative statements, through language the poet relies on symbols whose value is determined by relationships between sign and sign, sign and the outside world, sign and the hearers or speakers themselves. Like the limited language of mathematics, that of the poet may confine the values expressed in his language to his own interpretation. The poet, like the scientist, may then be bound by a restrictive mechanism which determines his observations and their expression.

Two generations have now passed since the publication of the quantum theory, generations in which scientists have deepened their findings and poets have pushed beyond their earlier restrictions. Some even beyond the bounds of natural human language. The proposed conference 'In Search of Reality' would explore ways by which scientist, poet, and student of language might overcome limitations in the pursuit of an ultimate reality.

Raja Rao and Winfred P Lehmann

## Indian Literature in Search of Form

Traditional Indian literature—whether the Vedas, the Upanishads, the Puranas, or the writings of classical writers like Kalidasa, Bana, and Bhartrihari, was the expression of a profound philosophical perspective (Vedantic) strictly formulated. In fact, this created the Indian psyche. With the coming of Western civilization to India, however, a challenging situation arose in which the traditional forms were quickly abandoned, bewildered as the Indian writers were by the newness of European concepts in poetics and the nature of the novel.

The contemporary problem is to try and re-establish the traditional form in response to the changing patterns of thought and society—a modern form, both for poetry and the novel. By taking three contemporary novels from three different Indian languages, I propose to show a possible form emerging out of this struggle. And indicate, just as the modern novel in both Europe and America is moving toward the poetic and the symbolic (Joyce and Robbe-Grillet), how India will come to treat the novel as an expression of myth—this the only possible expression of reality—thereby linking the modern problem to the tradition of the Puranas. Thus, the Indian novel would be both Indian and modern.

Raja Rao

# 15

# An Irish Interlude

The Irish sensibility is an encompassing one. It feeds on its obstacles with passion, with irony, with tragedy—'the heroine Deirdre feeding the hungry with her soul'.

There's a personalness to Ireland, an individual's *rencontre* with destiny. It has a vastness of imagination, and a tongue that seems made of bell-metal that rings with the depth of a cathedral peal. The whole country is human in a way no other nation is. Its peat fields, waterfalls, incoming bays, turreted hills, its ruins . . . Ireland's ruins are a history of emotions surrendered to time.

Its lakes seem so much a metaphysical in-turning that you half-expect them to wake up and talk, rise up and take a stride with you, or become as white birds taking a turn at a pool on flat Ben Bulben's top. For if you know this ancient rock formation at all, it's like a warrior in full knowledge of his victory trying to heal his desperate wounds, lying down after the battle, sword stuck in the earth, his breath piping through space over clear waters.

The Bay of Donegal is to its right, and the great poet, the greatest of this rock's children perhaps, lies at its feet, kicking at its heels. The poet, foolish man, had gone off to the Mediterranean and France to die—but Ben Bulben would have had him lie at its mountainous feet. And there he remains, the poet Yeats.

> Under bare Ben Bulben's head,
> In Drumcliffe churchyard Yeats is laid . . .
> Cast a cold eye
> On life, on death.
> Horseman pass by!
>
> W.B. Yeats

Yeats rests in a churchyard more like a drawing room (the living keep the Protestant churchyards trim), and he, who could inhabit the past, hears the sermons of his great-grandfather the clergyman, 'an ancestor who was rector there long years ago'. In the churchyard is a Celtic cross that seems to whirl life into space, turning the 'drawing room' into a house of supernal judgment.

Ireland itself looks like a Celtic cross, which explains why it is mountainous all around and an empty plain in the middle. God makes rare things in His image. Ireland is in His image—hence the Cross; Deirdre, Mother of Sorrows; and poetry. Poetry in Ireland does not seem the privilege of the intellect, but the leaping tongue of the hedge, the sparrow, the stream of Connemara, the ringed silence of Kerry, the light of Clonmacnoise, the metallic ingredient of the Irishman's speech.

The Irish roll their words as if to change them into acts, and are so frightened of these, their own vocables, that as if defending a castle of yore, they pour molten metal on the heads of their fellow Irishmen. And then laugh. The Irish tongue laughs at all men, or weeps when necessary. 'For if you've sorrow,' said the teacher Arland Ussher, 'all Ireland's on your side.'

The author Sean O'Faolain remarked, 'In Ireland it's in bad taste to be serious. You have no heroes in Ireland but were you to have one you must laugh at him, too.' One day in the halls of Trinity College, Dublin, Frank O'Connor, talking of his dead elder, Yeats, laughed so much and made those listening so full of gaiety, they wondered, like in those cultures that do not weep at death, if they weren't at a festival. The Irish ever talk of death, and so laugh it away. And drink does the rest.

Yeats did not appreciate death in the same manner; he was too grave a gentleman, too particular about everything from his gestures and diction to the cut of his hair, the colour of his handkerchief, the tip of his boot-knob. He took himself seriously, his watchtower *very* seriously, building it against dampness and war—so that when the Troubles came and the British went searching for the rebels, Yeats stood with a red light by a broken bridge, warning nationalists of the danger. The waters gurgled harmlessly past, and Ireland's day was saved.

> And Parnell loved his country
> And Parnell loved his lass.
>
> W.B. Yeats

Ireland is like no other country in the world. It's a gem apart, something historic and holy that man has set aside for the sake of imagination, a country where the 'little people' still hold sway. If you've any doubts about this, you've just to sit by a stream or lie in a meadow contemplating the cloud-bannered hill, and suddenly the whole countryside will be peopled with little-folk not more than a foot-and-a-half high.

They seem to enjoy still the first privileges of man before his fall. They are as genuine as they are mischievous, from behind hedges will frighten you, make the evening air so crisp and transparent that you may see chariots drawn by bees, or the grasses individually stiffen and shine. It's all a question of your ability to perceive space; some only look as from a distance instead of closely, as at a jewel. Only when you look closely are all movements seen, and colour, and humanity.

Man is supercilious enough to think he alone inhabits the earth. But there are those older than he who have remained small. These, the fays, have no wish to scale the moon or read philosophy. They live among flowers and move without effort, think without a mind, yet are supremely knowledgeable of nature and her laws, of the waxing of the moon and the waning of the sap. The fays are charmed by ecstasy, which explains the puckishness of the Irish.

The infamous Black and Tans still hide behind the rugged hills of Connemara, the Connemara of shallow bays, many horses, and Richard Murphy, poet of Ireland by the grace of God, and son of the former governor of the Bahamas by the grace of His Britannic Majesty. Oliver Cromwell, too, still stalks Stephen's Green, the same Cromwell who hated the very shadows of the papist 'devils'. But the Irish are stronger than he or anyone, even Hitler. Their cross is the swastika become whole. Hitler kept it broken and became fiendish. But they with their monkish knowledge completed it, so instead of

Hitler you have de Valera. The Irish keep Satan himself at bay with whiskey, the wide sea and the charm of their Celtic cross.

This Cross is to Ireland what the Himalayas are to India: the source of wisdom, of defence, of prosperity. Indeed, sometimes of an evening on the Isle of Innisfree, you can lie on the shore and feel India in your bones. I often imagined Ben Bulben a minor emergence of the Himalayas, a western rampart of the Indian presence. And the River Shannon at Clonmacnoise, a western Ganges. On another day at dusk, I saw Shiva and Parvathi (or was it Krishna and Radha?) glide over County Clare in a chariot of flowers. And the fays, too, must dance somewhere on the Himalayan heights.

One night in Galway, I went to see the movie *Nine Hours to Rama*. The hall was full, the film dull; you wouldn't think so, it being about the assassination of Gandhi. Gandhi so admired the Irish, especially the great O'Connell. And with Annie Besant added to the Indian scene, a part of Indian history is forever wed to the Irish.

Also, in County Clare, the actress Lelia Doolan walked us over peat hills to visit Patrick Scott, the painter. This is where we first saw the fays. You could almost picture the poet and mystic AE walking up those bog hills, up and up to their top, where the little people showed him the throne of Krishna. The evening was Himalayan blue, and the music *malkauns*. Night would soon fall, and in the twilight, you could see AE rushing down, entering a hut, and by peat-fire composing this poem on Krishna:

> I passed before the cabin door
> and saw the King of Kings
> at play.

Tumbled upon the grass I spied
the little heavenly runaway.
The mother laughed upon the
child made gay by its
ecstatic morn.
And yet the sages spoke of It as
the Ancient and Unborn.

The fact is AE saw the gods; Yeats only felt them. As for that embodiment of Irish rebellion, Padraic Pearse, who'd read too much Tagore—he was hanged for them.

What could an Indian philosopher do in Ireland? For one, he could see nature—and men, the natural man, the man of ancient Greece but devoid of sexuality. 'Which is taboo in Ireland', one of its most illustrious sons said to me. 'Haven't you noticed?' No, I had not. There's a breath about Ireland that is holy, and I was carried away by this etheric fantasy that seems so ancient a part of man.

A fact is not the truth, as the wise George Berkeley, true Irishman that he was, proclaimed some three centuries ago. Fantasy is the recognition of the 'beyond-the-fact'. When a Queen Maeve is more real than Queen Victoria, you feel the beginnings of philosophical wisdom. And the recognition is joy.

# 16

# The Word

The language we write must equate our being. The stuff of every word we utter must be the essence of the object. Hence, the sound rounded is not the word; the thingless thing *shining* in it is the vocable. A word, all words, therefore, exist out of time. The time-bound word—and so language, as such—is never appropriate to any situation. The used word is dead. Truth is fresh. All words have to be made fresh, new, to go back to silence.

The vertical perspective is the only way wherewith to signify a real phoneme. The breath goes *up* to reach the unstruck sound, *anahata*. 'The phoneme is a somehow unmanifest form of sound—*avyaktanukrtiprayo dhvanih*—which shines in the rising of breath—*uccare*. Its nature is mainly that of the seed of emanation and reabsorption. By repeated exercise (on it) one enjoys supreme consciousness.'

अव्यक्तानुकृतिप्रायो ध्वनिः ।

—तन्त्रसार

*avyaktānukṛtiprāyo dhvaniḥ* ।

—*Tantrāsara,* Abhinavagupta

Therefore, poetry must be silent. Each phoneme fully uttered to itself creates no word, but a nameless name naming itself as pure being. Thus, literature becomes the universe; that is, each object in its proper state is the whole of sound, *sabda*—the totality of what is, just *is*.

And therefore, nothing happens. Literature, like music, must know itself finally as pure silence.

# 17

# The English Language and Us

The word arises from stillness, like an orchid from the Himalayas. People thereabouts say the orchid lives one hundred years.

The Vedic poets *saw* words, they did not invent them. From their Himalayan imagination arose the Vedas. The real poem is pre-existent, like the sculpture in a rock, the word as primordial as the sun and the moon. As the waters.

Saraswathi, the Goddess of Literature, hence the word, is also a river flowing from the Himalayas. She is, says the tradition, hidden underground, and joins the Ganges and the Jumna at Prayag, the earth's navel and the centre of sacrifice.

Sacrifice is the process by which one's self withdraws into the background and becomes *Purusha,* the Primal Man, *the* Self. According to the Rig Veda, this is what the gods did: they bound Him, Purusha, the Primal man, bound Him to the earth and sacrificed Him. Purusha as offering . . . the devas and gods performed sacrifice, and here sacrifice itself was worshiped as sacrifice by the gods.

यज्ञेन यज्ञमयजन्त देवास्तानि धर्माणि प्रथमान्यासन् ।
—ऋग्वेद

*Yajñena yajñamayajanta devāstāni dharmān iprathamānyāsan |*
—*Ṛigveda*

And from the sacrifice of Purusha arose the world.

From His, the Primal man's, navel came the mid-air,
From His head the sky was fashioned,
From His feet the earth, from His ears the quarters.
Thus, they formed the world.

Rig Veda, XC

Poetry then is the Self speaking of the Self, Purusha, to Itself. Hence, poetry *is* sacrifice. The poetic experience is a eucharistic rite. The concatenation of the precise word that is 'seen' is literature; the Vedic sages were called *kavis*, or poets. Poetry is prayer.

Jawaharlal Nehru was born at Prayag, where the Ganges, the Jumna, and the Saraswathi meet. He went to Harrow and Cambridge and wrote a chaste English prose which startled the Bloomsbury world. He knew the word and its meaning were inseparable, as Kalidasa says of the god Shiva and his consort Parvathi—of stillness and the expression of stillness. One must remember, since the word, *sabda*, vibrates from silence, its essence also is silence. From the word you go back to silence, from vibration to peace, *shanti*. That is Parvathi playing with Shiva and dissolving into Shiva.

To speak correctly, you must be rid of your mind, rid of the mediocrity of the flat plains. You must reach back to the mountain cavern from which, invisibly, inevitably, the river

Saraswathi rises. Water is anonymous; the river is water, the sea is water, the ice on the Himalayas is water. Every drop of these is water. Saraswathi says, 'My home is in the waters.' So now, let the waters flow.

Such is the tradition to which I was born. I did not go to Harrow. Or even to Cambridge, which I had visited and admired. I went to France instead, for I did not like the British, yet loved the English. Since the French treat their language as if it were primordial (the French Academy, after three hundred years, is still completing its dictionary), I learnt, in addition to my Vedic heritage, the French tradition. My English then was born of this very strange marriage, an incestuous marriage, for Sanskrit is in many ways the mother, or if you would, the grand-aunt of the Indo-European languages. From this incest, I became the creator *and* the inheritor. Indeed, writing in the English language, I committed incest twice over.

This is in the pure Indian tradition. In the great Upanishads, which are the ancient explications of the Vedas, it is said that *Prajapathi,* Lord of Man, is the universe, and Vac, the word, His sister. He united sexually with Her. She became pregnant. She then departed from Him, and produced these creatures, these words. She then entered back into Prajapathi, Lord of Man—hence Vac, the Word. Say the Vedas:

> It is I, like the wind, breathe forth,
> And set all the worlds in motion.
> Beyond the heavens and beyond the earth am I,
> And all this I have become in my splendour.

How to legalize, to normalize this incest is a grave question. It's not so much a moral problem (we Indians, like the Greeks, are not such great moralists) as an ontological one. Which, alas, is not an English itch. But Indians love and revel in metaphysics.

One must go back to the primordial purity of the Himalayas, go to where the words are truly *seen*. This requires a certain askesis. Being a Brahmin by birth, dipping *back* into myself is as natural as going *up* the Himalayas. At the foot of the Himalayas, at Hardwar (the door of Hari, or Vishnu, the Preserver), the water of the Ganges is incarnadine. When you plunge into it, then emerge, with the sun rising over the Himalayas, you can see the words carved in pure space. Of course, the sounds of the sanctuary, then of the Bengal gram venders, the betel leaf sellers, the sellers of sweets made of milk and mountain cardamom—all these could distract you with their singing. So sometimes I did not see clearly. In fact, I should say rarely did I.

It was then I fell from grace. Nor did the English dictionaries, even the best Oxford, help. It may amuse you to know that my father loved the English language and considered it holy. He even learnt Anglo-Saxon to go back to its sacred roots. So, whensoever I was in difficulty, I went back to my meagre Sanskrit, that the primary, Indo-European root prevail.

When in Africa once—the Africa of Africa, today called the Republic of Central Africa—I met a man amidst its tall, dark trees, on a wide, much-islanded riverbed. He was a Belgian digging for diamonds, living with a woman whose grandfather, or so he said, was a cannibal. This Belgian engineer, with his sophisticated consort, had been schooled by some strange destiny at either Harrow or Winchester. When in the course of a conversation we were trying to find the proper word for something, we went back to the sacred Oxford Dictionary, the shorter version. Finding the word, we saw that it reached back to its Sanskritic, Indo-European root.

I cannot recall what word we were discussing, but can remember the dark, oily Congo River, the still, high primary flora, the mythic speech its people wove as they lisped, shouted, and sang. I had to wonder how the French language could ever hope to exalt this antique earth, these Caliban trees, and the sky that seemed just a patch of cosmic belly. It was like the space between one's fingers—which, as my Belgian friend told me, cannibals loved most. Remember, our ancestors were at times cannibals; in Russia today, if Solzhenitsyn is right, men ate men at the Gulag camps. Yet, of that Stalinistic world was some of the world's great literature born, Pasternak, Dostoevski, Akhmatova, Mandelstam and others.

Unless we eat ourselves, symbolically, we could never write, or see the true linkage between words. Here I quote from a great African poet, Aimé Césaire:

> *le Congo est un saut de soleil levant au bout d'un fil*
> *un seau de villes saignantes*
> *une touffe de citronnelle dans la nuit forcée . . .*

Just as the Congo River spawned a Leopold Senghor or an Aimé Césaire, we, too, in India, writing in English, must recognize the goddess Saraswathi, invisible but ever flowing through us. The literature of Africa and India, respectively, can only come from the rhythm, colour, and stretch of the Congo or the divine Saraswathi. Our speech is made of the first sounds we hear, our imagination of the landscape we see. There is no art in India that does not imaginate the high Himalayas; we are an ambitious people. We have to make our words, see our words, as they simulate the august curvatures capping the non-temporal snows of the Himalayas. We are, with their great Olympus, like our cousins the Greeks. Or Dante, with his sweet innuendoes of the Florentine hills crowned with pines, on which pours melodious sunshine. I quote Dante:

> *E una melodia dolce correva*
> *per l'aere luminoso.*

We have to be authentic. The timeless has to be seen in time. Though I write for historical reasons in the English language (the language of Shakespeare, the only good thing we inherited from British rule except perhaps the police department), I must make my English speak Sanskrit. My language must speak the hills, the Deccan hills, and the wide Ganges, the changes she makes in her course, long and wide. We can only be epic, like the Russians were epic, with our parable islands, muddy or clear according to how the snows on the Himalayas melt or freeze—fierce and pure to begin with, then ending in a million wandering streams, each one a Ganga before settling into the sands of Calcutta. We have then to dredge into our dictionaries. And it's from these that they come, the 'ships' of all nations.

The only will that Jawaharlal Nehru left was a noble prose poem to the River Ganges.

Our prayers today are just being fashioned. The forms our literature must take are still being discovered. As Nehru often reminded the world, we are an ancient people, but a young nation. Our literature itself is ancient, like the rocks and the waterfalls in Wilson Harris's *Palace of the Peacock*. But we are also contemporary; as a French scholar of Indian philosophy once said, India is ever contemporary because she is timeless. There is a famous dialogue in the Rig Veda between the poet and the rivers; again, kavi means both poet and sage. The poet here is the great Vishwamitra himself.

> Down from the lap of the mountains, longing,
> Like two mares moving gleefully apart,
> Like two white mountain-cows with their calves,
> The rivers Vipas and Sutudri rush with their waters.

Then He, the poet, says to the rivers:

> Stop at my friendly words of request,
> Rest for a moment, observers of the Law,
> With a noble hymn, asking for their favours,
> The son of Kusika calls to the rivers.

And the rivers answer back:

> Do not forget, O poet, this speech of yours,
> Which after ages will be resounding.
> In your praise-songs, poets, be loving to us,
> Lower us not amid men.

Such is our task, a difficult one, but we must not lower ourselves. Otherwise, we will insult our rivers. We must see the Himalayan orchids, not plant Simpson pansy seeds in our Himalayan pots. Yet as modern biology shows us, using a Sanskrit graft we might create a subspecies of the English language, a vernacular like the American, or the Irish, or the Caribbean; we can never forget English is of Indo-European heritage. We'd hope whatever grows from this would live one hundred years, but who can tell? We are still in the stage of experiments. Alas, however, we have our Indian Lysenkos. These do not *see seeing*, and it is in seeing that all shapes are embedded.

I have spoken only of words here. One needs to know the stone before the temple is built. In fact, when the stone is found, the temple, as it were, builds itself. As do words. All temples in India are in the shape of the Vastu Purusha Mandala, the form of Essential Man. We can only shape that which we are. A work of true literature is that which dissolves back into that which created it. Form ultimately is formless. The Buddha says to His disciple Sariputra:

रूपं शून्यता, शून्यतैव रूपं ॥
—प्रज्ञापारमिताहृदयसूत्रम्

*rūpaṃ śūnyatā, śūnyataiva rūpaṃ ॥*
*—Prajñāpāramitāhṛdayasūtram*

Here, O Sariputra, form is emptiness, and the very emptiness form.

# 18

# Dissolution is Fulfilment

As the word and meaning ever flow, so do word
and meaning hasten toward You, parents of the
universe, Parvathi and Parameshwara!

वागर्थाविव संपृक्तौ वागर्थप्रतिपत्तये ।
जगतः पितरौ वन्दे पार्वतीपरमेश्वरौ ॥
—रघुवंशम्

*Vāgarthāviva saṃpṛktau vāgarthapratipattaye.*
*jagataḥ pitarau vande pārvatīparameśvarau.*
—*Raghuvamśam*

Dissolution is fulfilment. When the feminine principle,
Parvathi, dissolves into the masculine, Parameshwara, or
Shiva, action becomes non-action, and thus is creation. Where
infinity dissolves into zero is peace. When one dissolves in *true*
death, one is Nirvana, without 'being one'. The Buddha said,
'That which does not disappear has never been.'

What seems a paradox, therefore, is a clear statement of reality. For only where duality dissolves is reality; the Absolute can never be dual. The *Kavi*, He who has insight, gravity—*Agni, Angirasa,* a keeper of the herd, He that is light, the Kavi Kratu, the poet-sage of the Rig Veda—He it is who dissolves the objective world into its no-thingness. Where the subject and the object dissolve, that is where one is deeply one's self, *the* Self, where the word dissolves into meaning. Remember, the world was created by the Word. As Bhartrihari, the great sage of linguistics says in the first verse of his *Vakyapadiya*:

> *The Brahman, the Absolute, who is without beginning or end,*
> *whose very essence is the Word, who is the cause of the*
> *manifested phonemes, who appears as the objects,*
> *from whom the creation of the world proceeds.*

For, say the Vedas, first there was neither existence nor non-existence, from which existence arose. How it arose, who did it, did He know it—maybe even He did not know it. For when He who creates tries to know what He created, He is dissolved *into* that which He created, into that which is He. So there is no one left to say anything, nor anyone to say it to. Thus, we come back to the circle from which there is no escape. Could the circle ever conceive of an escape? No. What then the answer?

Truly reasoned out, the circle has never existed. Space goes into the make of the circle. When space is realized as space, even the lines of the circle are seen as the substance of space; there is no circle. All is Brahman.

This realization makes one dance. Encircled by the aureole, a halo of cosmic fire, Shiva dances on the illusion of time. When the subject and object dissolve, one is free. The Absolute seems far from here. But when the here is seen as *here*, you realize no here *is*. There and here dissolve into is-ness, pure Being.

'It is name as it appeared as form, and it is form which appeared as name', the Mantra Shastra says. The name of an object, the vibration of that object in pure space, *akasha*. So the sound is the object and the object the sound. Poetry is just that, the dance of the precise word; its metrics, its chants are cosmic laws.

There is a celebrated hymn in the Rig Veda called '*Purusha Saktam*', 'The Song of Man', one of the greatest hymns ever uttered.

> A thousand heads hath Purusha, a thousand eyes, a
> thousand feet.
> On every side pervading earth he fills a space ten fingers
> wide.
> This Purusha is all that yet hath been and all that is to
> be; . . .
> So mighty is his greatness; yea, greater than this is Purusha.
>                               Rig Veda hymn XC lines 1–3

Purusha, the Primal Man, first created the devas, the gods. These gods thought, what a fascinating thing it would be were they to sacrifice Him who created them. The sacrificial victim, Purusha, they sprinkled with sacred water, laid Him on the sacrificial grass, and cut Him into bits. Then they set fire to the grass, and Purusha was purely burnt. With Him as oblation the gods performed the sacrifice, also the angelic orders and the sages.

When Gods prepared the sacrifice with Purusha as their
offering,
Its oil was spring, the holy gift was autumn; summer was
the wood.
They balmed as victim on the grass, Purusha born in
earliest time.
With Him the Deities and all Sadhyas and Rsis sacrificed.

                              Rig Veda XC lines 6–7

The sun and the moon, the stars and the seasons arose then, even
the Brahmin and the warrior, the tiller and the moneymaker.
Also animals with 'two rows of teeth', cows, goats, and sheep.

The moon was gendered from his mind, and from his eye
the Sun had birth.
Indra and Agni from his mouth were born, and Vayu from
his breath.
Forth from his navel came mid-air, the sky was fashioned
from his head.
Earth from his feet, and from his ear the regions.
Thus they formed
The world.

                              Rig Veda XC lines 13–14

That's the way the universe came to be.

From that wholly offered oblation were born the verses
and the chants. From it arose the metrics, the rhythmic naming
of words; He the word, and they the objects named. The word
is the naming sound *and* the silenced sound; He, Purusha, is
Brahman. That is how ritual started. Fire dissolves objects as
intelligence dissolves concepts. The sacrificing of mind and

body is the true birth—the Knowledge of Brahman, the true
Brahmin, the twice-born.

Finally, sacrifice itself was offered back as sacrifice:

यज्ञेन यज्ञमयजन्त देवाः ।

*Yajñenaya jñamayajanta devāḥ.*

The circle is complete. From pure nothingness, *purnata,* fullness
remains. And from this silenced sound the word rises again and
falls back as meaning. The game goes on. And Shiva dances the
*tandava,* the rhythmic movement of creation and dissolution.
Shiva's Parvathi is simply amazed at this spectacle. She is
poetry, He the poet; the word is He, She the signification.
Only where the object dissolves is meaning, and *all* objects
dissolve in meaning. There is indeed but one meaning. The
Buddhist poet Saraha says:

> Word, word, words you use, O fool,
> But there is only one word which is the Word.
> And that has no name.

It's this nameless Word that is meaning. Every word in every
language, in the past and future, now and ever, must dissolve
to be meaning. There is nothing but meaning. All is meaning.
Knowledge, *jnana,* is That. And That is the I-principle, the
Atman, the Brahman. The Word, therefore, is 'I'.

The 'I' here, of course, is that which has no body or mind,
for even the body and mind are known only in the 'I'. As
Valéry said, 'When the ego self *(le moi)* is not, is the "I" *(le Je)'*.
That is *jnana,* Knowledge, not the known but the Knower, the

*jnanin*, the Sage. And the true poet is the Sage. The word that arises from silence goes back to silence; the word, the vibrance of silence:

मौनव्याख्या प्रकटित परब्रह्मतत्त्वं. ।
—दक्षिणामूर्तिस्तोत्रम्

*maunavyākhyā prakaṭita parabrahmatattvaṃ. ।*
*—Dakṣiṇāmūrtistotram*

Silence is the publication of the Absolute. The word, the substance of the word, is silence. The word *sabda* is silence. Sabda is *shanti,* peace, and shanti is *sukham,* happiness.

'It, linguistics, *vyakarana*,' says Bhartrihari, 'is the road to salvation, the remedy for all impurities of speech, the purifier of all the sciences, and shines in every branch of Knowledge.'

# 19

# The West Discovers Sanskrit

About the beginnings of the nineteenth century, during the Napoleonic wars, an Englishman found himself trapped in Paris. He could neither go back to his own country nor return to India, where he had his job. He had, however, while in that strange, rich, corruptible, oriental country, learnt an extraordinary language that seemed to him as no other.

As often happens with Indians, they claimed for their language (as for many other things there) superior qualities. It was, of course, the oldest and richest in the world—Sanskrit, which in the language itself means the 'together-perfected', the totally refined. The Englishman, like a few others, marvelled at its great virtues but could not quite endorse all the magnificence the Indians claimed for it.

The goddess Saraswathi, or perhaps the Englishman's karma, or maybe both together, had decided he would, for historical reasons, be detained in Paris and unable to proceed on his journey. Taking the opportunity this delay offered, he shared the ancient language with local scholars.

His discovery caught fire. People began to listen with much eagerness and attention. It was also, one must not forget, the time when German romanticism had its first echoes, and the myth of India, as everybody knows, played a decisive part in feeding the imagination of the German intellectuals. Important texts in Tamil were translated into Latin, then printed in Holland—these were the great Upanishads, originally composed in Sanskrit. Thus was the European mind fed in its karmic necessity by an imagined India.

When, because of the Englishman, Sanskrit itself came on the scene, so revolutionary was its discovery that scholars could hardly believe their eyes. Here was an ancient language which seemed linked with their own Greek and Latin and was perhaps older than both. This came as an intellectual shock to the proud European. The more people learned of it, the more they flocked to Paris—from Germany, England, even Italy—to study this new language. It was in Paris that the European school of Sanskrit scholarship began.

The more they learned, the more enthusiastic they grew, and simple translations of some of the better-known Sanskrit texts began to appear. By the middle of the century, the reputation of Sanskrit literature had grown so immense that few of the French poets, or for that matter the English, failed to hail Saraswathi or Lakshmi, Shiva or Rama. In France, these included Hugo, Leconte de Lisle, and Lamartine; and in England, of course, Shelley. Some scholars even concluded the introduction of Sanskrit the greatest event in European cultural history since the rediscovery, of Greek in the fourteenth century.

Because of its subtly, exquisite riches, and deep philosophical traditions, Sanskrit would soon become a major world language. By the third quarter of the nineteenth century, with Europe embracing Indian philosophy through Deussen, Schopenhauer, and Müller, it was to enter the mainstream of European thought. Nietzsche, at the moment of losing control of his mind in Turin, was found reading a *Purana*. Schopenhauer openly acknowledged the influence Indian philosophy had had on his life.

While this awakening to Indian thought continued— sometimes through purely scholarly works like those of Max Müller's, sometimes through sentimental and theosophical interpretations of Indian philosophy—politics suddenly came into the picture, delaying this Indo-European cultural communication. Two great wars would occupy the world to a degree that made scholarly exchange at the deeper levels difficult. However, as musicians in both Europe and America tell me, Europe's discovery after World War II of the marvels of Indian music was of great technical significance, even apart from the sentimental intervention of the sitar amidst the picturesque customs and costumes of modern-day youth.

I have said all this only to come to my central theme. When European writers and linguists fully unearth the metaphysics of the word—the Sanskrit tradition of it—they will realize what a magnificent treasury of human achievement lies buried in its texts. Nowhere else, not even in Chomsky's dream perhaps, is the word analysed to its roots in a manner which is as masterly in its imaginative scope as it is logical in its structure. The day the Western world discovers this Indian science of the word, it will lead modern literature to greater possibilities—as apprehended by Mallármé first, followed in part by Joyce, if without the philosophical background that the Indian tradition offers. The addition of this tradition would make the origin and effect of the word something more than an experience of linguistic adventure or intellectual accident. The word as such, properly understood, would become the very means of liberation.

The writer then becomes not merely an aesthete in the literal sense of the word but one dedicated to the search for the Ultimate Truth, Brahman. The precision of the word, therefore, becomes a *sadhana,* a spiritual exercise. The magic of Mallárme would still weave its wonders, the Joycean invention its rich immediacy, only not by a horizontal statement but a vertical one, something like Valéry was trying to perform. The Sanskrit writer knew the word had a finality that only a spiritually liberated man could name; thus did Mallárme's ideal poet and the poetic language of *Le Livre* already exist in Sanskrit. The key to it all was there for any serious poet to find. And put into practice.

What then is the word? In Sanskrit we call *sabda* both sound and word. A small dictionary I have defines sabda as: 1) sound, the object of the sense of hearing; the property of *akasha,* ether. 2) the notes of birds and men, etc.; noise in general. 3) the sounds from musical instruments. 4) a word, sound, or significant word, as in titles, epithets, names.

From where does the word arise? From silence, of course. For before the word was, there was silence, and after the word, silence again. From this silence arises an intimation of some feeling as yet nameless, a feeling applicable to all words of whatever nature. This unnamed feeling, which silence pushes up, now enters into the realm of the mind, and there becomes a picture. This picture is then articulated as sound-silence, which finally the tongue postulates as a flowing note, short or long. This note is heard by someone through his ear, the message then traveling to the brain and into the realms of mental awareness, from where it again descends into primal silence. There it dies—and where the sound of the word dies into silence, understanding arises.

Only in silence is the word understood, it is from silence that it arises; from one silence to another is communication made. Here we have to be very subtle. The question is if anyone, anybody, is present where absolute silence exists. Or could there be two ultimate silences? Since where there is silence there can be no formulation of thought, there can be no person, as all silence is impersonal. That is beyond the personal. And beyond the personal there is nobody. Hence there *is* something where the sound first emerged as a possibility, but no person. That *something* where there is no one cannot be different for different people—differentiation is itself the result of the person, of the mind. Where there is no one, but 'is-ness is', we find both the origin and end of sound. And of the word.

Let us look at it from another viewpoint. The Western dictionary defines the meaning of sound as the object of the sense of hearing. In Indian tradition, however, as opposed to this, the object is that which comes into being *because* of the act of seeing and has no independent existence, or *drishyam*. In fact, since nobody can separate one from the other, there is no seer separate from the object seen. So is it with sound. There is no hearer separate from the sound, the hearer and the sound are one. How then can one say one has seen an object, one has heard a sound?

Now, what then is the world? The world is just a playful division for one's enjoyment of one single experience. The *rasika* is one who delights in *rasa,* the flavour; the enjoyer of artistic experience is he who has a taste of the Absolute. Hence is sound nothing but the Absolute Itself, the Absolute in terms of the poetic experience. It is *Sabda Brahman,* the Absolute as sound-word.

If the Absolute then is the origin and the end of the word, both the grammarian and the poet are *sadhakas,* men who practise words as a means to liberation. Bhartrihari, our great poet, not only created some of the most exquisite verse ever written in any language but also a textbook on words showing the way of liberation, *moksha,* through the Word. Here we meet Abbé Henri Brémond's demand of *prìere poésie,* except there is no God in the Indian outlook on poetical experience; Brahman is none other than oneself as silence. I enjoy the Word for myself, and this enjoyment is poetry. If a person has the intellectual maturity and artistic sensibility to do likewise, then we both appreciate the same thing. But never is there a two—rather ever and always a not-two. Even to say 'one' would be blasphemy.

The word at this level is naturally magical. The real name of anything is its vibration in pure silence, in ether, *akasha.* The perfect word is the vibration of the object by itself, in itself, and about itself, where no one hears, sees, smells, tastes, or touches. The perfect word rightly pronounced would then have the power, at a slightly lower level, to create the object itself. No word that is not a natural name of any object, thought, or experience could be its precise definition.

Poetry then is that magical link of precise names only understood when you have the possibility of that silence within you, where the word goes back to its silence and you enjoy Brahman, the Self. Which is to say there is only Joy, with no one there to enjoy it. Joy joys Itself.

Brahman, of course, is *Ananda*, pure Happiness. Such is the origin and aim of Sanskrit poetry. Our first Vedic texts tell us from the very beginning that our poets were sages, *rishis, kavis*. The Vedic poets laid the foundations of Indian civilization. The kavi was the seer. Hence wisdom and poetry are one, the word become mantra, sound as incantation.

An ambitious tradition indeed. Beginning at three or four thousand B.C. and lasting until at least the seventeenth century, a tradition the Sanskrit poet maintained throughout, enriching the world with some of the most astonishing combinations of sound and meaning man has ever created. Kalidasa, our most important poet, coming almost two thousand years after the Vedic rishis, commences one of his most famous poems with the verse:

वागर्थाविव संपृक्तौ वागर्थप्रतिपत्तये ।
जगतः पितरौ वन्दे पार्वतीपरमेश्वरौ ॥
—रघुवंशम्

*Vāgarthāviva saṃpṛktau vāgarthapratipattaye.*
*jagataḥ pitarau vande pārvatīparameśvarau.*
—*Raghuvamśam*

What he is saying is that just as sound goes into the make of meaning and meaning into the make of sound, so do Shiva and Parvathi, Shiva being the masculine principle and Parvathi the feminine. Without Shiva there is no Parvathi, just as without the word there is no meaning.

The word made concrete is the object, the feminine. Hence *padartha,* literally the meaning of the word, which today has come to represent an object, any object, an eggplant at the market or the stone on the street or a complex trituration of a doctor.

The sound made object is the world. But as there are so many objects, and of such complex natures, how does one achieve the naming of objects? For this, the Vedic poets, the seers, had already shown the elements to have primary sounds, or root sounds—'ra' for fire, and so on—which means that every element, when you take the world as a possible reality (always a problem with the Indian), has its own vibration, and each sound its own colour, its own geometrical form. With colour, sound, and form combined, the word must structurally represent the whole of the object's qualities.

To compose an object, since there are so few primary elements, the root sound, or *bijakshara,* must be added to another root sound, and these to yet another. The composed object then combines itself with other objects, or actions (which, as you *see* activities, are also objects) to make a whole phrase. Because of its associative value no phrase can stand by itself; when one group of root sounds joins with another you have a whole picture painted in one sentence.

This sentence, as are many of the eighth-century poet Bana's, might be two pages long. Joyce would not have had to invent his very private language had he known Sanskrit— and with root words joined to other root words, a whole book such as Mallárme's *Le Livre* could be but one sentence. Though this has yet to be achieved, someday someone might.

From the structure of so complex a philosophy of the word, writers developed many theories of poetics, the most important being the schools of *rasa, dhvani,* and *sphota.* The word rasa, again, means flavour, or enjoyment; 'dhvani' means sound-suggestion, aura; and 'sphota', the quantum of any word—it explodes. The poet, through a complex organization of sound—sounds that create objects—works up an associative structure of images and vocables, level by level, which when rightly pronounced and rightly heard (from silence to silence) leads you to ultimate happiness, the Absolute Itself. Though there are eight rasas in all, some believe nine, it does not matter whether the prevailing mood is love or hate, tenderness or harshness; you can reach the Absolute through any of these modes of being.

Total hatred leads to the abandonment of the world, total love to the surrender of the ego. Every emotion leads you to the Absolute, for it is to Brahman that every gesture and sound is directed. Hence all poetry is worship made to the Absolute, to Shiva Himself, who is none other than the Ultimate 'I'. All words are worship offered to the Self; and mantra, or incantation, nothing less than supreme worship offered to the One, more accurately described as the Not-Two, *ekan, advaiyam*.

Having come this far, you will realize how impossible it is to translate Sanskrit prose or verse into another language. The vocabulary in Sanskrit is so rich that words like 'rainbow', 'king', or 'mistress' each has over two hundred synonyms, and Shiva, Devi, or Krishna over a thousand names. Since the language is so supple in structure, you can begin your sentence almost anywhere, and yet it be light, precise.

Though I said translation from Sanskrit to any other language is impossible, this is not entirely true. If all words are worship, and since true worship is universal, any language can lead one to this worship. He who comes to the silence within himself will find the proper equivalent, in any context, for each of the Sanskrit words. The world is rich enough, and man inventive enough, to find multiple combinations of sounds that say the same thing. Each experience, however, is unique, differentiated, and new. Such is the majesty of all true poetry, in any language. Indeed, if Sanskrit poetics could be rightly understood and applied by critics, it would open a new understanding—from the very depths of one's being—into the meaning of any book, prose or verse.

Going back to Kalidasa's simile that word and meaning are as Shiva and Parvathi, She, as its meaning, arises from the word to go back to the root of the word, Shiva's silence. The Indian poets have played a grand game of sounds and sound combinations. Nowhere have I found the rasa of poetry as I did in Sanskrit. The ends of true poetry are stated to be profit, pleasure, virtue, and liberation. Let us take a few examples:

देवी सुरेश्वरी भगवती गङ्गे ।
—गङ्गास्तोत्रम्

devī sureśvarī bhagavatī gaṅge ।
—*Gaṅgāstrotram*

*Devi:* one who shines, she is lit, a goddess.

*Sureshvari:* from the word *sura*, meaning a higher being. *Ishwari* implies the head, but with a woman as chief.

*Bagavathi:* she who is blessedness, ever generous.

*Gange:* the Ganges.

This verse translated could read:

You the chieftain, or queen, of all the superior beings,
   or gods, and blessedness itself—you the Ganges.


त्रिभुवनतारिणि तरलतरङ्गे ।

*tribhuvanatāriṇi taralataraṅge ।*

*Tribhuvana:* the three universes, three fields, three gardens.

*Tarani:* heaven, but also the sun, a ray of light, a raft, a boat.
Tarani is also close to *tarangita*, which means waving, tossing
with waves, a leap, or flowing clothes.

*Taralata:* trembling, waving, tremulous, fickle, libidinous, sparkling.

*Ranga:* colour, hue, dye, paint, the theatre arena, dancing,
singing, nasal modifications of a vowel.

These definitions, as you can see, could have no real translation,
for each word has several meanings and any single level of
meaning leads you to one proper statement only. Whereas it's
possible to end up with at least four or five statements without
difficulty.
    But word by word, at a horizontal level, you could
translate the verse as:

    O Goddess or Lit-one, queen of superior godly hosts,
        blessedness as flow, O Ganges. O you flowing,
          floating, shining through the three universes,
            and making the space, the arena, to dance on,
                flow on . . .

काशीक्षेत्रं शरीरं, त्रिभुवनजननी व्यापिनी ज्ञानगङ्गा.

*kāśīkṣetraṃ śarīraṃ tribhuvanajananī vyāpinī jñānagaṅgā.*

*Kashi:* Benares. It comes from *kash*, to shine, to be brilliant, beautiful. Kash also means to see, to appear, to banish, or to open, bring out, bring to light. Benares then is when you are brought out, your true nature shown—when Shiva, the Absolute and Lord of Benares, who is yourself, *the* Self, shines in His true splendour.

*Kshetram:* field, ground, soil; place, abode, repository, sacred spot. Place of pilgrimage, a sports ground (for Shiva dances here), the body as the field where the soul works. Also, the mind, the house, a triangle, a diagram.

*Shariram:* a body. The constituent elements. That which is made of all the elements.

*Tribhuvana:* again, three universes, three gardens, or fields.

*Janani:* mother, mercy, compassion, the great Mother.

*Vyapini:* pervading, filling, occupying; coextensive, invariably concomitant. It is also a name of Vishnu, who sustains the world by pervading it.

*Gyana:* supreme knowledge. Knowledge for liberation.

*Ganga:* The Ganges.

This verse may be translated as:

> In the shining field of the body flows
> the three-universe-pervading Ganges-as-Knowledge.

The last example I give will again be from Bhartrihari, prince, grammarian, and poet, who was outshone in brilliance only by Kalidasa.

मातर्मेदिनि तात मारुत सखे तेजः सुबन्धो जल
भ्रातर्व्योम निबद्ध एष भवताम् अन्त्यः प्रणामाञ्जलिः ।
युष्मत्सङ्गवशोपजातसुकृतस्फारस्फुरन्निर्मल-
ज्ञानापास्तसमस्तमोहमहिमा लीने परब्रह्मणि ॥
—वैराग्यशतकम्

*mātarmedini tāta mārutas akhe tejas subandho jala*
*bhrātarvyoma nibaddha eṣa bhavatām antyaḥ praṇāmāñjaliḥ ।*
*yuṣmatsaṅgavaśopajātasukṛtasphārasphurannirmala-*
*jñānāpāsta*
*samastamohamahimā līne parabrahmaṇi ॥*
                              *—Vairāgyaśatakam*

*Matar:* mother.

*Medini:* earth, land, soil, place.

*Tata:* father, someone worthy of respect. Also said in affection, but never with familiarity, as papa.

*Maruta:* air, relating to maruts, the spirits of the air; breath, vital air.

*Sakhe:* friend, copain, companion, soother of pain, one to whom you can fall back on for help or enlightenment.

*Jyotih:* fire or light, the light of Brahman, the faculty of seeing.

*Sabandho:* duly bound together, well-bound, or fraternally united. Also means father, husband, or charged with fragrance.

*Jala:* dull, cold, frigid; water, or a libation.

> The first line, therefore, could read:
> O mother earth and father air,
> O friend fire,
> great kinsman, water.

I conclude this talk quoting the verse in full so you can see how poorly it translates.

> O mother earth and father air
> O friend fire, great kinsman water,
> Brother ether—to you all
> In final parting, I offer reverence.
> Through your long associations
> Have the right deeds been performed.
> Through you I have won pure, shining wisdom,
> Unweaving the sweet delusions of the mind.
> Now I merge in the Supreme Brahman.

And Brahman, as we have seen, is pure shining silence.

## 20

# The Cave and the Conch: Notes on the Indian Conception of the Word

वागर्थाविव संपृक्तौ वागर्थप्रतिपत्तये ।
जगतः पितरौ वन्दे पार्वतीपरमेश्वरौ ॥

—रघुवंशम्

*Vāgarthāviva saṃpṛktau vāgarthapratipattaye.*
*jagataḥ pitarau vande pārvatīparameśvarau.*
—*Raghuvamśam*

So said Kalidasa at the beginning of his famous *Raghuvamsam*, the lineage of the Raghus, meaning the lineage of Sri Rama— Sri Rama, the great hero of the *Ramayana*.

The verse simply says, 'Just as word and meaning are one, so are the sacred couple, She, Parvathi, and He, Shiva, the Lord of Lords.' Of course, there's a more subtle meaning to it. For, Parvathi was the daughter of the mountain, and so She, born to the mountain, was the child and essence of the Himalayas. He, Shiva, was an ascetic, clad in tiger skin, who sat always in meditation on the Himalayas. She, the word, the sound, was the vibrant activity of the mountain. That is, She was the expression of monumental silence. But He, Shiva, was Himself the silence. Thus She, fell in love with the unmoving, She Herself, pure movement. She, the daughter, He, the Father—He the Lord, She, the Beloved. Literature, then, the concrete expression of this marriage.

They had one son, Ganapathi, the Elephant-headed God, whom one lauds at the beginning of every worship. He, the Lord of obstacles, who removes all obstacles. He, the critical faculty, which erases the accidental, the unworthy. In this way, literature becomes true, sacred. The word and meaning become one, they dissolve into the background, the unobstacled, the holy writ which is not written, but is *seen*. The poet the *seer*. Hence the sage.

The true poet, he who chants the unspoken word, *para*.

Then comes the word, visible, formulated. This formulated word, *pashyanathi,* turns into *madhayama*, the sounding word. Finally, we have the objectified, the vulgar phonemes, the commoners' utterances, *vaikhari*.

We Indians are obsessed with the beginning and the end. The great fourth-century sage Gaudapada says, 'What is at the beginning and the end is also in the middle.' There is water in the pond, which is unmoving. There is water in the river, that moves. But finally, there is the ocean. So, water remains water, always.

What then is the origin of the word, of *sabda*, sound? Since before speech there was no sound, and after the sounding of the word there is no sound or word, the background of sound is silence. Not a lack of sound, but rather the womb of sound, from which, arising, the sound goes back to its own reality. The self of sound, then, is again silence. And silence is Brahman, the Absolute, the Uncreate. Creation is the seeming daughter of silence going back to the Mountain Lord. The feminine principle returns to the masculine when both then are dissolved into their essential nature.

But why should silence become sound? It's because of *lila,* the playfulness of nature. Lovemaking is play. Thus, silence playing with its expression, is sound. The enjoyment of this lovemaking is *rasa*, the aesthetic joy of the unmanifest rising to manifestation, only to go back to its own background. Thus the circle is complete, and nothing ever happens, just as waves go back to the sea, reaching back to their source, water. When sea and wave realize they are both water is the moment of true enlightenment.

Liberation, then, is serious play. The writer plays with *self,* as word, with words.

* * *

The word rises also to name things, that is, to name thoughts and emotions. 'Objects are there to be named,' as Rilke said. The conch, for example, is the silence of the sea, made concrete. The wave is only the conch in preparation. So are all objects the essence made concrete. To name them properly one must see them in their own beingness. You cannot name them if you cannot know them–that is, *be* them. I cannot name the tree, if I cannot know the tree, and the knowing is the merger of the object in the subject. Therefore, the object finally is 'I'. It's only as 'I', playfully, that one names objects, just as a child makes a doll into its daughter by pure appropriation. Or again, the word rises as *Udbhava-murti*, the image or idol that often rises of its own accord from my inner earth, my ground—in consciousness—and I discover it there, as the legends say, of many of the idols in our sanctuaries.

The sanctuary is a series of shrines. The book, the true book, is like those caves of Ajanta or Ellora, or Elephanta, sheerly arising in the silent rock. Upon entering the caves, you see in the rediscovered faint light a Buddha, gently bent and holding a lotus in his hand. Or a Shiva, on whose head the Ganges pours, which He ties in the knots of his hair.

Such is the Indian tradition. The discoveries of Ajanta and Ellora were possibly contemporary to Kalidasa. The shrine is already in the rock. Or the Udbhava-murti already in the ground. Remember Mallarmé and the perfect book.

Silence is not the lack of sound, but the active interregnum between breaths. Silence the conch, whose inner breath, the *pranavam*, the *Aum*, as the texts say.

'Aum, the word, is all this.'

ओमित्येकाक्षरमिदं सर्वम् ।

*omityekākṣaramidaṃ sarvam* ।

# Part III

# The Interviews

# 21

# I Write for Myself

## An interview by Ranavir Rangra

Ranavir Rangra: **We often hear that one can express oneself better in one's mother tongue than in any other language. But you chose to adopt English as the medium of expression for your creative writing. What was it that led you to make this choice?**

Raja Rao: I would have liked to express myself in Sanskrit. It is the richest language in the world, a most sophisticated language. You can use it, play with it, anyway you like. But I am afraid my Sanskrit is not good enough. Though my mother tongue was Kannada, I was brought up in Hyderabad, so it was not good, either. Nor did I think it sufficient for my intellectual perversities. I needed a language that I knew better than Kannada, and that was English.

This being said, I have tried to reshape the English language for my own needs. I refuse to write English like an Englishman or an American. Therefore, my English, as people have told me, is rather unusual, but I try to be authentic with regard to what I write. When I talk of France, for instance, very often I think in French; when I talk of Mysore, I think in Kannada; and when of Delhi, I enjoy thinking in Hindi, though mine is not good. I believe it is a question of what you want to express and how sincerely you want to express it.

**When you write on Indian subjects, your homeland especially, you must be, as you say, thinking first in Kannada then translating to English. Is that not a cumbersome process?**

But I write very little about my native Mysore. It was only in the beginning that I wrote some short stories about Karnataka. I've spent the years writing mostly about northern India, Europe, and America.

**Do you have any particular type of reader in mind when you write in English on Indian topics?**

I have no readers in mind at all. I write for myself.

**Not even to fully convey to the reader what you want to express?**

I take writing as a *sadhana,* a spiritual sadhana. That is why I write so little and take so long a time to complete my text.

**This reminds me of the Srimad Bhagavad Gita, which elevates literary sadhana to the level of *tapa*,**

**calling it *vangmaya,* or literature *tapa.* Do you write in longhand or give dictation?**

I used to write in longhand, but because of poor health, I now lie in bed typing on a small bedtable. My first impressions are mostly written in longhand. My first novel, *Kanthapura,* and the early short stories, were almost always in longhand.

**Let's go now to your novels *Kanthapura, The Serpent and the Rope,* and *Comrade Kirillov.* I find they are in first-person singular, the narrator being 'I'. From this, I gather there must be some autobiographical element in them. Take Moorthy of *Kanthapura,* for example. How much autobiography does he represent?**

I like to write in the first-person because I find it much more sincere. Gandhiji used to say that you can lie to someone else, but you can't lie to yourself—to yourself you must be sincere. I think that is the reason why I write in the first-person singular. But this 'I' is not always autobiographical. During the freedom movement I was not in India, but Europe. Once, Nehru asked me, 'Where were *you* in prison?' 'I was never in prison,' I replied. So only something of me is there in the novel.

**Let us discuss two of your major female characters, Madeleine of *The Serpent and the Rope* and Irene of *Comrade Kirillov.* Both women love their husbands very much, but the husbands, Rama and Kirillov respectively, are mostly silent about their feelings, and to their wives appear dispassionate. Perhaps this**

**nonresponsive attitude of theirs creates doubt in the minds of the women. Madeleine decides to free Rama to marry an Indian woman, thinking he would be happier with an Indian wife.**

**As for Irene, in addition to her husband's aloofness, she was sure that the moment Kirillov's foot touched his land, India, he would start hating Europe, despite all his talk of internationalism. She highly disapproved of this double standard of his. In contrast to her husband, she hopes their son Kamal will love the *whole* of humanity. Does this mean that Indian men, despite the concept of *Vasudhaiva Kutumbakam* (the whole world is one family), cannot prove worthy husbands to their European wives?**

The European does not usually have the Indian's depth of sensibility. So in a certain sense, any marriage outside one's own background creates problems. I would say that these problems are many—thinking, eating, sleeping—and all present their own particular difficulties. We are a sophisticated race of people, which often even the best of Europeans are not. In terms of daily living, we may not seem so, whereas in terms of thinking we are highly sophisticated. When an Indian man has a dialogue with a European woman at the intellectual level, he may like it, but it is not as easy to live it. Even in India today, marrying outside one's community creates problems because different people have different backgrounds. How much *more* difficult is to marry a woman from a faraway country? The Indians view marriage as *dharma*. But unless both people have fully reached this understanding, dharma will be on one side only. The woman may not think in terms of his Indian dharma, but hers as it relates to her background.

**Is it because of this that Rama of *The Serpent and the Rope* says that one should not only wed a woman but also wed her God? In both this novel and *Comrade Kirillov*, we know only the women's reactions when it comes to love, while their husbands remain silent.**

There is a difference between man and woman. A man, particularly the south Indian, is an austere person. We are not that sentimental. Rama is very much a south Indian. He is always rather distant.

**It appears Rama's attitude of distantness was sensed by Madeleine. Is that why, despite her earlier confessions that she loved him, she later questions herself with, 'Do I love him?'**

That is very European, too. In the West, people doubt themselves a great deal. They are sure of things in the beginning, but not later on. So it was with Madeleine; though certain of her love at first, later she would come to doubt it.

**Why was it that Madeleine decided to free Rama so he could marry another woman? Did Rama give her cause for this?**

This question has been asked of me many times. In a marriage as sensitive as theirs, divisiveness comes from a deeper level than its mere expression. Many things in life seem done without rhyme or reason.

**Would you say they are done intuitively?**

No, even deeper than intuition.

**What is your concept of love? We come across a definition in the novel: 'To be free, one must know one is free, beyond the body and the mind; to love, one must know one is love; and to be pure, one must know one is purity'. Here, I am interested in your concept of love. Will you please elaborate on this with reference to Rama and Madeleine?**

This concept is of *Advaita Vedanta*. Love is beyond Rama and Madeleine. It is a state; Europeans fall in love, but that is not love. Love is one's intrinsic nature.

**Do you mean that it is a spontaneous and not a conscious act?**

It is not a conscious activity. It is one's real nature.

**In the Sahitya Akademi meeting the other day, quoting Bhartrihari, you said, 'If a writer is not seeking *moksha* through his work, he is not a writer.' When asked to define the word, you said, 'Moksha is to establish one's Self beyond body and beyond mind.' In this way I think, every writer, even unknowingly, attempts this through his work. He establishes himself in the word. Even when**

**dead, when his body and mind have ceased to exist, does he exist in the word? Is that what you mean?**

No, I am not talking of that level.

**Can you elaborate on this?**

By beyond the body and the mind, I mean being completely impersonal, beyond one's personality. Beyond *Mana,* the sensory mind; *Buddhi,* the intellect; and *Ahankara,* the ego.

**Do you mean beyond ego?**

Yes, mind is ego.

**When we say *sadharanikaran,* or common cause, from the reader's point of view do we mean 'beyond ego'?**

When I'm writing, I don't care a damn for the reader. I try to say something for myself, and if that is interesting to me, it might interest the public. I don't think of the public as such. Maybe that is why I write difficult books. My new book is very difficult.

**Is that your new novel, *The Chessmaster and His Moves,* which you expect to be published in a few months?** [Ed: *The Chessmaster and His Moves* was published in 1988.]

Yes. However, let me add that I am not interested in the author, the publisher, the royalty, the reviews, etc. These things don't concern me.

**But surely you must be interested in communicating?**

Communication for me is that which gets communicated *to me*. That's all.

**But isn't there a reader within the author also?**

That reader is myself, not outside myself.

**Unless the reader in you is satisfied, can you be satisfied?**

I don't think the reader within is *ever* satisfied.

**Thinking of it in that way, no author can be satisfied completely. Is it this feeling of inadequacy—that what he wanted to say he has not been able to—which prods him to write again and again?**

No, it prods him to correct himself. Constantly.

**To perfect himself?**

As far as possible.

**You have very successfully depicted female psychology through Madeleine in *The Serpent and the Rope* and Irene in *Comrade Kirillov*. Some say that male writers are not able to do justice to their female characters, as they create them from a male point of view. Do you think there is any substance to this contention?**

During the creative process, when one goes beyond one's body and mind, one is neither male nor female.

**Do you mean that at this level of writing one rises above gender? And what of caste?**

Yes, beyond all limitations—if one can reach that level. I only aspire to this state.

**Another thing being discussed these days is an author's commitment. It is often said that every author must be a committed one. If so, to whom or what do you think a writer should commit?**

I cannot say about others, but I am committed to Advaita Vedanta. I am a *sadhaka*.

**Do you think you are committed to Advaita Vedanta at the conscious level, or because that is your real nature? Can you please explain?**

Yes, I can! When you understand that beyond your body and your mind is the Absolute Reality, then you are a *vedantin*.

**I noticed that in your novel *The Serpent and the Rope*, you relate an ancient story about Krishna, Radha, and Durvasa to explain this point.**

Yes.

As the story goes, Radha becomes highly possessive of Krishna. Krishna, wanting to enlighten Her, looks for an opportunity. In the meantime, Durvasa Rishi arrives, and pitches himself across the raging River Yamuna. Krishna asks Radha to cook some food and take it over to the Rishi. Radha asks Krishna how to cross the swollen torrent, who then instructs Her to tell the river that Krishna, the *Brahmachari,* is asking it to give way to Her. Radha thinks that Krishna is lying—how could he be a Brahmachari? She knows better than anybody else this is false.

On hearing Krishna's command, the river gives way. After Radha feeds the Rishi and is about to leave, he asks Her to tell the river that this time it is Durvasa, the *Upavasi,* who wishes it to part for Her. Now She thinks the Rishi is also telling a lie—how could he be an Upavasi when he has fed himself with such utter satisfaction? But on hearing Her command, the river parts.

Radha is completely baffled by what She sees as a new reality. On returning to Krishna, she questions Him about it. He asks her who is the Krishna whom she loves? Is it the Krishna of the body, or of the mind? Then tells Her that unless she loves Krishna *beyond* His body and His mind, Her love is an illusion.

It is not an illusion. It is a misunderstanding.

**A misunderstanding of what?**

A misunderstanding of the Truth, Advaita.

**Some say that spiritual growth can take place only in duality and not at the Advaita stage. When God the Creator was bored with loneliness, he created the universe. *Eko Aham Bahu Syam,* the One manifests as the many.**

*Yes,* but that is *lila,* play. When you are only one, *the* One, there can be no boredom or problem of any kind. You enjoy yourself in your loneliness.

**Did you at any time write poetry?**

No, never.

**But given your mind, wouldn't poetry come naturally to you?**

People tell me my prose is poetic.

**That is correct. No prose is a hundred percent prose, and no poetry is all poetry. Good fiction usually has a poetic element.**
**Now we come to literary awards. How do you view them as a writer? Do you think they encourage writing? And by that, I mean genuine writing.**

Awards are irrelevant at my level of writing. When the Sahitya Akademi award was announced for *The Serpent and the Rope,* I wondered whether any of the judges followed one-tenth of what I was saying in the novel. I thought of refusing it straightaway, but my sister made a point against such a move. She asked me whether I was getting too proud of myself to accept an award. I thought maybe she was right, so I consented to receive it and attended the function, but purely as a ritual. However, I asked my friends not to come.

**Would you like to say something about your forthcoming novel, *The Chessmaster and His Moves*?**

No. I don't want to precondition you. Wait and read it.

**Has the book something to do with your concept of love as illustrated in your earlier works?**

It does even more so, I hope. But again, wait and see.

**What are you writing these days, or are contemplating?**

I am correcting my earlier writings.

**For new editions?**

These are not published. I am working on some of my unpublished material.

**I ask this because experience has shown me that some writers in their attempt to improve upon their earlier work have spoiled it.**

That is possible.

**Can you name any of your works, or the characters in them, which might have brought about a change in your outlook on life? I venture to ask this because I**

**feel that not only does the writer create his characters but they also create him. Without his being aware of it.**

I understand the question, but it does not apply to me personally. I create change in me by my sadhana.

**But sadhana is not done at the conscious level, is it?**

You begin with it at the conscious level.

**But isn't sadhana a continuing process involving many rebirths, and one picks up threads from previous lives to continue growing from them? It is my understanding that the sadhaka does not consciously bring about change in himself.**

I am not consciously aware of the change taking place in me at the deeper level. All I'm saying is that it is my sadhana that changes me, not the book.

**By sadhana do you mean all that you experience in life?**

No, it is something special. Meditation, if you like.

**Have any of your short stories or novels been translated into Kannada or any other Indian language?**

A collection of my short stories, *Raja Rao ki Kahanian,* has just been published in Hindi. People have tried to translate it into Kannada, but they say it is not possible because of the originality of my style. Some tried, but none succeeded.

## 22

# A Conversation with Raja Rao on *The Cat and Shakespeare*

## An interview by Ayyappa Paniker

Ayyappa Paniker: **I noticed you have a subtitle for *The Cat and Shakespeare*, 'a tale of modern India'. I found it almost as intriguing as the main title. What exactly do you mean by modern? Does the book deal with recent events, or is there another significance to the word?**

Raja Rao: By modern, I mean a new version of an old tale, and when I say tale, I mean fable. It is an old story in a modern setting, a story as ancient as the Vedas. But I wanted the reader to realize it is not something new, though the characters seem to be.

**Going back to the main title, the connection you make between the cat and Shakespeare probably involves a puzzle, the cat representing the Indian**

**consciousness or awareness of the world. How do you relate the cat to Shakespeare?**

First, let me explain why I chose Shakespeare. It has been revealed to me that Shakespeare was a sage, a word I rarely use. The difference between the cat and the sage is the sage is a being who has no ego, while the cat represents the impersonal principle. The cat in this case is a she-cat, a female, a being of compassion mirroring the male. The male cat is the *pure* impersonal. Shakespeare, of course, being a sage, could only have an impersonal view. The cat, therefore, reaches back to Shakespeare, who in turn absorbs the cat into himself. The two are one.

The main point of the book is the question how does one behave after one has realized the impersonal principle, the Truth? One behaves a-logically, not illogically, not dramatically but simply, one's actions impersonal but full of love. One also sees many meanings in a single action; thus, does a-logicality reveal a state of being beyond cause and effect. There are three levels involved: the logical life sequence, the a-logical meaning of the logical life sequence, and the reality which is beyond logic and a-logic.

**When you mentioned the cat was female, I was reminded of the Malayalam word for the female cat, *chakki*, which is derived from the Sanskrit *sakti*, a form of *parasakti*, that which looks after all creatures. I was delighted to see that your cat embodies the mother image—she as mother of everything and not just a personal goddess.**

That is the concept of *Jaganmatha,* and because in the novel I am talking of Kerala, what you say moves me deeply because in a sense I wrote it without knowing this fully.

**Which brings us to the novel's locale. Trivandrum has been the setting of two famous novels in Malayalam, both historical, the more recent in Tamil. I think for you, however, the locality has no importance geographically. Is the story's location in Trivandrum in some way significant to its allegory?**

As you said, this is an allegory—a poem, or a fable. Compare it to the three floors of a house: the first is the a-logical, historical, geographical reality of Trivandrum. The second is its allegorical reality, the third the Absolute Reality. In other words, the waking state, the dream state, or the deep-sleep state. This last, like the sky, covers everything, the whole reality.

**Do you regard reality as a dual concept? I was very much interested in the double image of the novel's characters Govindan Nair and Ramakrishna Pai. I'd say that between them, they represent two parts of reality. My doubt is that dualism has any role to play in this. Is there a way of going beyond this phenomenon of duality? Could your Guru's notion of objectless perception, for instance, be related to this?**

No, for me it is poor Pai, who is only an Arjuna, while Govindan Nair is Sri Krishna. One is the 'man-man', the other is 'man-beyond-man'.

**Coming back to the story, I want to say I was not a little pained to read about the death of the boy in the novel. I don't say his death was arbitrary, not at all. But you did make him, as seen through the eyes of the girl, a fully developed human being. Then, just as I began to take a personal interest in him, you snatched him away. Do I have a grievance?**

Your grievance (laughs) should be against life because that's how things happen in the world. Plus, it depends on how you look at it. The boy dies, as you say, but for the remainder of the novel it is as if he has not died at all; his presence is stronger than when he was living.

The understanding of death as a purely phenomenal reality has to be transcended into the *presence* beyond death, the Ultimate Principle. The girl worships the boy as an absolute. And how can anyone say he has not himself experienced *the* Absolute?

**Is the concept of death in your writing, i.e., the way death is accepted as part of life's reality, related to the concept of the serpent and the rope? I'm not sure if one should accept the notion of maya as explaining away the phenomenon of death. Though in *The Cat and Shakespeare* there is no specific emphasis on maya, how in your view is the problem of death resolved?**

Maya is just the misunderstanding of reality, and the symbolic meaning of the wall in my novel represents this misunderstanding. Ramakrishna Pai could at any time go across the wall but was afraid to, fearing he would never come back. We all know that once we leave our personality, we cannot come back; there is no personality left (laughs again) after you go beyond it. So, I think it is the ego's game of trying to survive, suffering the miseries of *samsara,* rather than transcending itself and living a full life. Because beyond samsara is the fulfilment, *not* the denial of life.

Govindan Nair lived a complete life, playing with it, for to him it was play, *lila.* But poor Pai . . . how he suffered with his wife, his child, and so on! This is true also in the case of the unfortunate Iyer, I forget his whole name. I am referring to the asthmatic, miserable Iyer in the ration office, on whose head, humorously, the cat comes and sits.

Bhoothalinga, that was it. Bhoothalinga Iyer was a symbol of orthodoxy, dead orthodoxy. So he *had* to die. Whereas Govindan Nair was non-orthodox, an authentic man. The cat as the active aspect of reality killed orthodoxy.

**Govindan, whom you make a ration-shop keeper, shows the intriguing way you have grounded the Ultimate Reality in mundane reality. This is very effective in presenting the notion of life as *lila*. Nair, without making any fuss, without putting on the clothes of a yogi, achieves it. This is also, I think, another way of grounding Reality with a capital 'R' in reality with a small 'r'.**

I'm glad you saw that, because if the Ultimate Reality is not *the* reality, it is not worthwhile. To become a *sanyasin,* a supposed sanyasin like Bhoothlinga Iyer, is orthodoxy. If that is reality, life is not worth living. Govindan Nair shows that he can *live* the Reality, in the here and now, despite the ration office. That to my mind is his great success.

The Christian characters in the book, though, John and Abraham particularly, rarely talk, and when they do they seem to have a different understanding of things. They are not merely victims of life; they are operating on a lower level.

I wanted to show also, without forcing the issue, that Abraham represents Christian love, a 'higher-than-thou' attitude, whereas Govindan Nair personifies a 'higher I', the *Atman*. Something far beyond the Christian. Meanwhile, the Muslim in the story shows another aspect of human love, one of friendliness and compassion. Nair's love is not compassion, whereas the Muslim's comprises friendship, comradeship, decency. Nair, like Krishna in the Mahabharata, has gone beyond any human value.

**We should not leave out the female characters, especially Santha and the little girl Usha. Santha undoubtably satisfies all the requirements of the female principle. But at the same time, like most other characters in this novel, is she operating on two levels?**

I'm glad you brought up Santha. For me, I have always felt, as shown in *The Serpent and the Rope,* that man is a lonely and rather solitary creature. Pai rises to his higher self because of Santha, and she, with her devotion, humanity, simplicity, and truth, typifies the Indian woman. Her worship of Pai makes her more authentic than Pai himself, which is very often what the Indian woman does.

In all my novels, one of the things I've always tried to show is how the woman is more real and human than the man, as man is an abstraction of himself. There would be no war if women were in charge, as war itself is an abstraction. In fact, even Govindan Nair is an abstraction in that he is almost indifferent to the consequences of what he does. Santha, however, is not only concerned about consequences but, in worshiping a man, she makes a man a man (laughs).

Something vital for you to remember is I wrote *The Cat and Shakespeare* in Trivandrum. This is the only book—no, I've written one more in Trivandrum—the only *published* book I wrote there.

**I think as a Malayali and a citizen of Trivandrum, we owe you a great deal in correlating this reality with a small 'r'—Trivandrum—to that of the large 'R' of the Eternal City of Reality.**

Thank you. But allow me to close by saying that Trivandrum *is* Vaikuntam—and beyond!

# 23

# Indian English: Sensuous and Silent

## An interview by Yogesh Gondal

Yogesh Gondal: **What would you say is the essential theme of your novels?**

Raja Rao: Philosophical quest. Metaphysical quest. I will not use the word 'spiritual' because it has many meanings. The term 'metaphysical' is more appropriate because metaphysical means going beyond the body.

**Yes, but even so, your output is far too little for a professional writer. I have a feeling, therefore, that you don't really view yourself primarily as a novelist, a feeling which is strengthened by the themes and subjects of your later novels.**

In a sense you are right. Because my primary interest in life is to be a *sadhaka*. My spiritual life, my metaphysical life, my writing, my human life—they are all one. I can't divide myself, and therefore can't really say I am a writer only.

Indeed, I'm not a professional writer in that sense. But there's no other expression for me except writing. After all, Tulsidas didn't say he was a poet. Was Kalidasa a professional writer? Their tradition is my tradition.

**But at that time there was no question of anybody becoming a professional writer because there was no such thing as a publishing industry.**

Nevertheless, I belong to that period. If it can be said I belong to any period, it would be to the fourth or seventh century A.D. Should you ask me where and when I would be most happy, I would say India between those centuries.

**Although you have visited India quite frequently, aren't you more or less settled in the West?**

I am not settled anywhere. And if I am, it is India, in my depth rather than outside.

**But haven't you spent your entire adult life abroad? You left India for France at the age of nineteen.**

Yes, I have spent half my life abroad. But I don't feel that I have lived abroad. It's a very strange thing. I would come back to India from Europe and sit before my mother when she was meditating. And she would tell me, 'You look as if you were never gone.' Personally, I don't think being abroad has made any difference in me, to what I would have been if I had stayed here.

**Has living in France helped you in coming to terms with yourself?**

Oh, of course, of course.

**In a way that living in India would not have?**

Oh . . . (a long pause). France made me realize how truly Indian I was.

**How would you compare the contemporary intellectual and literary climate in India with that of Europe and America?**

I don't know enough about these things because I live a very solitary existence. I read little modern literature, almost none of the contemporary Indian, British, or American writers of the last thirty years. If I read anything, it's either philosophy or history. Or if fiction, I go to the Russians, Dostoevski and Tolstoi.

**But what about the intellectual climate generally?**

Well, every time I come to India, I see more and more of what one could term 'intellectualism', at least in the modern sense. In the last few days, for example, I've found much more intellectual life here than there was ten years ago. By intellectual life, I mean a preoccupation with ideas which are neither metaphysical nor philosophical, but analyses of situations.

**Would you say that by and large Indian intellectuals, writers, and thinkers are honest to themselves and the country?**

If they were, India would not be what she is today. First of all, most of them think in terms of Western modalities. They are preoccupied with Western values; very few of them are concerned with traditional Indian values. I once attended a writers' meeting in Calcutta where people were discussing Mallarmé and Rilke and so forth. Mallarmé, as you know, has no relation with India today.

**One of your primary concerns as an Indian novelist writing in English has been the problem of style, and the need to make the English language a suitable instrument for communicating the rhythm of Indian life. In fact, in the foreword to your first novel *Kanthapura*, you said, 'The tempo of Indian life must be infused into our English expression, even as the tempo of American and Irish life has gone into the making of theirs.' Do you think that Indians writing in English today have succeeded in moulding the English language into that instrument?**

Today, I would not use the word 'tempo'—I would say *rasa*. The *rasa* of India should go into the making of Indian English. On this trip to India, I have been extraordinarily impressed with the quality of its journalism; the country's journalist today is writing an English that has more of an Indian sensibility. The English English is a shy language. The American English is a language of pure statement (I'd almost call it unimaginative), but it is authentic in terms of its factuality. In contrast, Indian English is sensuous and endowed with silence.

**Would you agree with the statement that Indians are by and large more concerned than Westerners with the auditory effect of words and language?**

Yes, I think you're right. Perhaps that is why they are sometimes so pompous.

**But don't you think that this preoccupation with sound effects must also have had a healthy influence on Indian English?**

Yes, certainly. But I would put it this way: the Indian seems almost to embrace the word, whereas the Englishman shies before it and the American faces it. As if facing a wall.

**Don't you think this comes from the rhythm of some Indian languages, especially Sanskrit?**

Oh, yes! The auditory effect of Sanskrit in particular is the highest of all. As I said to you last week, I would have liked to have written in Sanskrit. It is the most wonderful language in the world.

**Would I be correct in saying that Sanskrit is your model for creating an Indian English?**

I admire Sanskrit so much that perhaps this has happened to me unconsciously. In fact, now that you mention it, if I find an English word used inaccurately in a sentence, I go back to the Sanskrit word I would have used.

**Ever since you started writing in the Thirties, you have been trying to evolve an Indian form of the novel. What is the model you had in mind?**

Except for writing in English, I would like to continue the Sanskrit tradition, which includes Hindi, Malayalam, and so on.

**Yes, but which literary form in the Sanskrit tradition are you trying to adapt the novel to?**

The Puranas. Let me tell you something, the success of Indian film has been a remarkable thing. People complain, 'But the films are too long, they're rubbish, they're mythological, the songs are all wrong!' But that is the Indian mind. And just as Indian cinema is finding its own way, we Indian novelists writing in English must find ours. I'm not bothered at all if structurally my novels don't follow the Western style. The Russians didn't think of the novel in the English manner, nor did the French.

**What, and who, have been the major influences in your life?**

In the beginning the greatest influence on me was the traditional literature of India. But all my life I have been on a great spiritual quest. This quest took me to Ramana Maharshi and Gandhi, to Benares and Haridwar, and many other sacred places and spiritual people. In 1941, I gave up writing because I knew that unless I found what I was looking for, I would never write again. Ultimately, my quest took me to my Guru, and it is my Guru who is now the greatest influence in my life. In fact, my Guru alone is my *only* influence.

**May I ask who your Guru is?**

Not yet. But I may tell you on my next trip to India.

# 24

# An Interview with Feroza Jussawalla
## and Reed Dasenbrock

Feroza Jussawalla: **Though all of us have ties to India, we are talking today in Austin, Texas, this representing the increasingly international and multicultural nature of the world. But many Asian and African writers are suspicious of this internationalism. The Indian poet R. Parthasarathy believes that a writer should write in his native language only. What is your sense of this? What is the role of the writer in today's multicultural society?**

Raja Rao: I am not interested in the general picture but only in my own personal experience. I don't consider myself multicultural; I am totally a Brahmin and an Indian, from India. I believe that you remain basically faithful to your own self—to your genetic and psychological background, the bio-psycho-sociological self.

**And this is true despite the increased contact between cultures around the world?**

Yes, it only took living in Europe for one week, when I was nineteen, to realize that I was an Indian. Part of my Indianness is my honesty not to parade under a guise that I am not. Despite multiple cultural contacts, I feel more Indian than ever.

At the psychological level, there is the collective unconscious of history. Traditions are only the reprints of psychoanalytic patterns of human thinking and being, a position I don't think anyone can quarrel with. Genetically, people do not change much; sociological and political facts pale before the deeper genetic realities.

**Is it hard communicating this sense of Indianness to readers of different cultures?**

I am not interested in communicating across cultures. I am what I am, an arrogant Indian. Some people have called me an Indian imperialist. India's greatness lies in its capacity to absorb.

Reed Dasenbrock: **What then of communicating to a reader not from India, such as myself?**

Writers do not communicate; this is a very misleading word. Writers have nothing to say. They experience.

**And provide the reader with that experience?**

Yes, if the reader is interested. But writers are not as attuned to their audiences as you suggest, as your word 'communication' suggests. Writing is an aspect of living. I am first a human being. My writing comes out of myself and continues to mature.

F. J.: **How *does* a writer mature?**

How does a human being mature? By going deeper into himself. That is the Indian tradition and, again, I am entirely Indian. I am more concerned with what Indian metaphysical and literary traditions say.

R. D.: **Would you acknowledge any indebtedness to Western culture?**

The most important of the West's contributions are psychoanalysis, genetics, and quantum physics. But the university atmosphere in America, for example, is too centred on books, not experience. It is encyclopaedic rather than interpretive. What is sad about the modern intellectual is that he is becoming a generalist.

**Are there any contemporary European writers you admire? Czeslaw Milosz, for one, has written a poem about you, *To Raja Rao*—the only poem he's written in English, I believe.**

We met in Paris and again in Austin. We mainly discussed how to address life, and though he and I differed, he was honest enough to accept the differences.

F. J.: **What differences?**

He believes in evil, and I don't. For a good Christian, evil is concrete. For a good Vedantin, there is no evil. In the Indian tradition there is none.

**But what about differences in India? Indian culture is hardly one entity. Isn't it multicultural in a sense?**

Why are you so interested in multiculturality?

**As a Parsi, it is natural for me to be interested in the expression of many cultures.**

But India is essentially Hindu. I have been to Parsi marriages, where the traditions are similar to the Vedic.

R. D.: **But if this is so, why write in English?**

I would liked to have written in Sanskrit. I have said this many times.

**Then you would have had a much smaller audience.**

Yes, but it would have been the right language in which to express my metaphysical and psychological experiences.

**Why don't you write in Sanskrit then?**

I have studied Sanskrit for many years but don't know the language well enough to write in it. Though I think I'd have written much better in Sanskrit.

F. J.: **What about your mother tongue, Kannada?**

My Kannada was never adequate. Though I was born in a Kannada-speaking area, I was brought up in Hyderabad, where they primarily speak Urdu and Telugu. Also, when I started writing, Kannada as a language needed to be modernized. I was too impatient then, but some of its writers have since gone back and modernized it.

When Indian writers ask, as they often do, why I write in English, I say, 'I am sorry. Historically, this is how I am placed. I'm not interested in being a European but in being myself. The whole of the Indian tradition, as I see it, is in my work.' In other words, there is an honesty in my choosing English, an honesty in terms of history.

R. D.: **Have you then never written in Kannada?**

Yes, I have. I have written a novel in Kannada, some twenty-five years ago. But I translated it into English, and it seemed much better.

**Has it been published?**

No, not in either language. [Ed: *The Song of Woman, Narigeeta*, was published in Kannada in 2012.]

**How exactly was the novel improved by translation?**

In English, it seems as if one can do what one wants with the language. As it's a newer language there are fewer rules, therefore more freedom for invention. I lived in France for a long time and know French almost as well as I do English, but this freedom is not available in French at all. It is a very strict language with little room for change.

**Have you written anything in French?**

Only a few essays.

**But *Comrade Kirillov* was first published in French, was it not? Was any of it written in French?**

No, it was translated from the English. But I did write the novel *in* France.

**Did you have anything to do with the translation?**

No. The translator was a close friend of mine, but I didn't help him with it. In any case, as he was so good, I didn't have to.

**The reason I ask is that there has been a good deal of question lately about the status of translations by the author. For instance, Czeslaw Milosz (whom we just mentioned), Isaac Singer, Vladimir Nabokov, and others have translated or co-translated their work into English. Do these translations then belong in English literature?**

I don't think that works very well. A certain authenticity is lost in the translation process.

**Yet you were just saying that you translated a novel from Kannada yourself.**

Yes, but it belonged to English, not Kannada. It wasn't something I had taken to a finished state in one language, then re-created in another. In each language, there are some things that are easier to say. I hope to write my last novel in Kannada, as it has certain shades and delicacies of expression that aren't available in English.

F. J.: **But you've said before that when one dies, one prays in one's own language, and that you would pray in Sanskrit, not Kannada.**

Seventy percent of the important words in Kannada are Sanskrit. When Gandhiji said 'Ram Ram' when dying, that was Sanskrit, not Gujarati.

**You have talked, and written, about how we come to know reality through language. What about all the different languages in India? Does this mean there isn't a common Indian consciousness?**

The differences in Indian consciousness are small. All Indian languages are born of Sanskrit, except perhaps Tamil, which is thirty percent Sanskrit. I think those who speak Indo-European languages tend to think alike. Indians, for instance, are closer to the Europeans than they are to the Chinese.

**Do language patterns condition the way you write?**

Again, some things can be said more easily in one language than another. This is true with Kannada, especially the silences.

**Is this more important in oral or written cultures? There is a lot of discussion now about the 'oral tradition', which, of course, you draw on in your novel _Kanthapura_. Do you think orality is the same everywhere?**

Oral traditions are similar because most are concerned with love and death. Here again, we are talking too much about internationalism and interculturalism.

**Has the tradition of the oral tale itself changed as a result of cultural contact?**

_Kanthapura_ shows exactly that.

**In Africa people gather as before, but sometimes give voice to tales in English. Or read from contemporary works.**

In India, those who read _Kanthapura_ can do that. But India already has enough wonderful stories. Why then would people want to share the story of _Kanthapura_?

R. D.: **Could you see yourself writing in Kannada here in Austin?**

No. I find I must be hearing the language to write in it, hearing it in the streets. When I go to France, it takes me a day or two to adjust and switch to French. The same is true when I return to India.

**In tracing the languages that you know and could have written in, we are moving into an area of particular interest to me. I'm fascinated by multilingualism. One of the questions I'm seeking an answer to is why so many good writers in English seem to come from the margins of the English-speaking community. And in many cases, English is their second or third language.**

Why do you think that is so?

**I wanted to ask you that.**

No, I'd like to know your answer first.

**I know of two ways to explain this. After modernism, British and American writers, particularly American, were so caught up in formal experimentation that they forgot they had anything to say. Form was all that counted in their work. Contemporary third-world writers by contrast, and for a variety of reasons, have a great deal to say.**

**The second explanation is that having English as a second language, or as one among several languages, is somehow an advantage because it makes the writer the master of the language, not its slave. Some feel that to learn a language well enough to write in it, one must speak it from childhood. But in this century, the best writers often come to English from the outside,**

**and that seeming disadvantage is really an enabling force. Do you think that coming to English as a second language has helped your work?**

I don't agree with either explanation. The important thing is not what language one writes in, for language is really an accidental thing. What matters is the authenticity of the author's experience, and this can generally be achieved in any language.

F. J.: **It's interesting to hear the word authentic linked to a defence of writing in a second language. Usually, in non-Western literature, it is an argument used by those insisting that one should return to writing in one's mother tongue. Ngũgĩ in Kenya, Parthasarathy in India, Kunene in South Africa—have all said that authenticity requires writing in one's mother tongue.**

For me this has not been true. They are right, however, in that one must stay in touch with one's language.

R. D.: **Both aforementioned African writers would push it much further. They feel that Africans writing in English is simply a mistake, that the minute one does so the language imposes its forms. And what emerges can only be colonialist in expression.**

I can't speak for African writers.

F. J.: **I am sure they would extend this to the Indian situation as well.**

But here we are, post-Joyce, and Joyce was very daring, very creative. We must now all be daring and do what we want with the language we choose. After all, T.S. Eliot and Yeats did not write like Wordsworth or Tennyson.

R. D.: **But can't that in turn become a new trap, the trap of becoming experimental at all costs?**

Yes, but remember, authenticity is everything.

**It sounds as if you would agree with the suggestion that having English as a second language is an advantage and this is why the best writers in English are increasingly neither English nor American.**

My answer would be that England and America are industrialized societies, and therefore have a very superficial culture, what one might call a 'horizontal' culture. They have lost touch with themselves—with a deeper, spiritual dimension of themselves. It is only out of this deeper experience that great literature arises.

Some great writers from the West, however, retain this dimension. Dylan Thomas had a genuine spiritual sense, as did, of course, Gerard Manley Hopkins. Eliot's search for religion accounts for much of the depth of his work; one could say the same for Yeats, with his unusual spiritual seeking. I am not speaking here of organized religion, but of the search for the transcendental. D.H. Lawrence revealed this in his work, even though he subscribed to no orthodox religion.

**And eventually he left England?**

Yes, which was very important for that aspect of his work. It is hard to be truly spiritual in a country like modern England. Who, except for Kathleen Raine, writes authentic poetry in England today?

**Is that why Lawrence felt he had to get out of England?**

I think in his case it was mostly the class system; in England, he was never allowed to forget he was a miner's son. So he married a German woman, an aristocrat, as not only a way out of that situation specifically but the industrialized world in general. France has less industry than England, or rather it modernized later, which is why the writing there was better than in England—Levi-Strauss, Foucault, Hugo. Though today this isn't as true.

**Is that why Beckett went from English to writing in French?**

No, I think it was because his work was too close to Joyce's. He could get away from Joyce by writing in French. Beckett, however, is a special case. Once more, it helps to hear the language you're writing in. After all, when Rilke lived in Paris, didn't he write in French?

**But didn't Joyce write *Finnegan's Wake* while living in Paris?**

Which is in another language entirely, isn't it? I didn't know Joyce well, but I knew lots of people who did. Joyce, incidentally, wanted to be a musician—that is his struggle for honesty, the music in his work. Honesty is the equation that joins experience and expression.

**What is the future of English in India? Are Indians likely to go on writing in English as well as in Indian languages?**

It is important to note that Indians are good at writing in other languages. They wrote in Persian, you know, for hundreds and hundreds of years.

**Yes, but now they've stopped.**

I am not much interested in the question of how long we will write in English or any language. How long does *anything* continue when judged in the long perspective of civilization? We are here now, and later someone else will take our places. I can't worry about whether Indians will use English in the future.

**But at present, do you think English is losing ground in India?**

Not at all. The English we use in India today is a much better English than it was some forty to fifty years ago. Then it was Victorian English; it is much more interesting, much freer now than it used to be. Indeed, most of it that I read in Indian magazines today is *very* much better. Some of it is worse, of course, as the standards of education have fallen. But when the British left in 1947, only one percent of the population could speak English. Now it is three percent.

**But Indian *writing* in English? Creative writing?**

I don't read much contemporary literature, from India or anywhere. Most literature today is pure form without contexture, which is why I am not interested in it.

F. J.: **Can there be such a thing as pure form?**

In a sense, there cannot be. If I had to describe a stone, the texture of the stone and that of my poetry must be the same. The experiencing of an object must include its texture. A man whose writing has both texture and form today is Wilson Harris, but a good deal of modern literature is simply journalism. I prefer to read the classics.

**How should we define the classics?**

Whatever speaks of realities, not supposed realities, interests me. I read the classics because of their concern for the fundamentals; otherwise, they wouldn't endure. I would much rather read a great spiritual writer like Dostoevski or Valery than what is written today. Why read a superficial novel when I could read the Mahabharata, or Shankaracharya?

R. D.: **Read it in Sanskrit?**

Sanskrit on one side and English on the other. That way when I am tired of Sanskrit I go to the English, and vice versa. There is infinitely more to the Mahabharata than what is being written today.

F. J.: **Do you think the Mahabharata could speak to today's American college freshman with any immediacy?**

If he is sincere. I saw Peter Brook's contemporary play, Mahabharata, in Austin. All classics are contemporary in that they speak of our essential relation to love, life, and death. This is true of the Western classics as well as the Indian ones.

**Could you name the classics that are key to you?**

*The Odyssey, Tristan and Isolde, Genji* in Japan, Chinese classical poetry, and, of course, Indian literature of every age. The revival of old Greek myths in the contemporary literature of France is very important, too.

**Is the cultural context also important?**

There is no cultural context to love, life, and death. Hamlet is universal, Orpheus, Oedipus—these are the fundamental myths of man.

R. D.: **What of the writers of your generation in India? You are from the same area in India as Narayan. Do you know him?**

I see him whenever I am in Mysore; we are good friends. But our work is very different. He writes of the social world, I do not. I am interested in metaphysics, in the Vedantic search for Truth.

**But don't some critics see Narayan's work as metaphysical?**

Metaphysical? I don't see how. There is a complex sense of social irony in his work, but I don't see any metaphysics.

**And Mulk Raj Anand?**

I know Anand very well also, from London. He, like Narayan, is interested in the social world, in changing the social world. I am not.

**So can we make a distinction between you and G. V. Desani on one side as writers interested in the Indian spiritual tradition, and Narayan and Anand on the other?**

Yes, but there is also a distinction between Desani and me. I know him too, as I brought him to Texas, where we both taught philosophy and still live part of the year. He was born in Kenya, I was told, outside the Indian tradition. I was born inside it, where I have largely stayed.

**But there is an irony here. Of the more philosophical of the four Indian writers mentioned, you and Desani both live outside India, while Anand and Narayan remain there.**

Anand also lived in England for many years. But that is irrelevant, mere chance. I could have easily stayed in India all my life. I happen to be in America because I was invited here, but it doesn't matter to me whether I am in America or Argentina. What does matter is I am in India, the depth of India. And I do not mean geographically.

F. J.: **You have said, 'My India I carry with me.' Would you say you're in India now?**

I am always in India.

R. D.: **How old were you when you went to France to attend university?**

Nineteen.

**At that point, was going overseas still a big thing, it involving sailing over the black waters, losing your Brahminhood, and all that?**

Yes, at least for the older people.

**Did they oppose your going?**

Of course! But then I was continuing our Vedic tradition, even in France. Tradition is not static; it is an absorption of deep human experience into a contemporary context.

**So after a time, did they come to accept it?**

Yes, they did, because I never broke with tradition. Which is another difference between Desani and me.

**Have you seen Desani lately?**

No. I think, you know, he is a Buddhist monk, living in great solitude.

**Where was he before you brought him to Texas?**

In India. Sitting on a hill in meditation.

**What do you think of contemporary Indian poets?**

I don't know much of their work. The best Indian poet I know is Parthasarathy. He is capable of tremendous work.

**What of A.K. Ramanujan?**

He is a very fine translator, very fine indeed. I only disagree with his choice of translating text into Western forms.

F.J.: **In your judgment then, there is a problem in attempting to mix Western and Indian forms. Is there a place for multicultural authors such as Zulfikar Ghose and Rushdie? Will they ever be considered classical authors?**

Honesty can always produce a classic. If gifted, a man may create a classic by being honest to himself.

**Writers like V.S. Naipaul and Ghose—how are they to manifest themselves?**

They need to find their self-nakedness; the Self has no nationality. Some writer friends of mine declare themselves French, but essentially, they are Jewish. I don't know if you are familiar with Freud and his *Psychopathology of Everyday Life*, but it contains great truths. As does his *Psychology of Early Life*. Without Freud there would be no Joyce, also no Proust. After four thousand years of persecution, the Jew remains a Jew. There is great esoteric meaning in this. In my new novel, *The Chessmaster and His Moves*, I try to paint a picture of the Jews who perished in the gas chambers and one who escaped that destiny.

R.D.: **The Jewish people and their culture seem important to you. Did you know many Jews in India?**

No, just a few. Among them the Jewish poet Nissim Ezekiel.

**What do you think of his work?**

It was very clever. But too Westernized for me.

F.J.: **If you were to lay out a formula for Indian writers to avoid the superficiality you've described, what would that be?**

Be honest.

**About what?**

Yourselves.

**Where they stand historically?**

No, within themselves. In *The Serpent and the Rope*, I do talk of history. But history is only politics deeply assimilated. I am concerned with man and his sufferings.

**Are life, love, and death part of suffering?**

Suffering and escape from suffering. And happiness—love is happiness. In terms of life, death, and immortality, I am interested in the fundamental questions: 'Who am I?' and 'What am I about?' In French, *l'amour et le mort*.

**And why is *love* essential?**

When you love, you become deeply yourself. All objects are known only inside yourself, even the one whom you love. Love is a way of knowing yourself. Loving is pure self-realization.

**And how is that important to living?**

Being oneself *is* living. Gandhiji said, 'If I don't live the truth, I am not nor ever will be free.' Being free enables one to express one's true self, *the* Self. This is moksha—dharma and moksha—and they are what interest me. Dharma is the honesty of oneself with oneself.

**Where does one find the words to describe that?**

Honesty creates the word. But what you don't say in life is as important as what you do say. The full stop is silence; hiatus in poetry is silence. The universe is vibrant silence.

**In India, when people are sitting together, often they are silent.**

I was married in France, and when I brought my wife to India she was shocked at the silence. When we visited the houses of friends they'd sometimes just sit there and say nothing. In India, behind the chatter, there is silence.

R.D.: **Yet sound, or at least voice, is also important in your work. Much of *Kanthapura* reads as if it were translated from Kannada; the syntactic patterns are those of Kannada, though the work is in English. Was any of it translated from Kannada?**

A very small part was written in Kannada, but most of it in English.

**Did you sound out those sentences in English, the ones that have Kannada syntax in them?**

Only in the sense that I heard the language in my head as I wrote. Sound is very important to me; in my new book I have many meaningless words that are just sounds, invented to be part of a Jewish liturgy.

**So Judaism is important in the new book?**

Yes. The book was first called *The Brahman and the Rabbi*. It ties everything together, the Kannada that was so important in *Kanthapura* and the Sanskrit and French tradition of *The Serpent and the Rope*. In *The Brahmin and the Rabbi*, I become universal.

F.J.: **What do you see as the differences between** *Kanthapura* **and** *The Serpent and the Rope*? **And what accounts for these differences?**

They differ the more authentic I became—that is, in the expression of my authenticity as it grew. The level of thinking also changed, matured. There are about two levels to *Kanthapura* and eight to *Serpent*, though no one has yet written of the eight. It is also a politically liberal work, but this subtlety escapes people. Most writers and readers today do not have the patience for depth. Writers tend to explain something already there rather than express something original.

**But what about the accessibility of literature to the common reader?**

I'm not in the least interested in that. The people who wrote the Vedas didn't say, 'Would the common man understand?' Not everybody understands Shakespeare, but that doesn't mean he wasn't great. Greatness comes from being yourself in your depth, not from your egocentric self. Depth permits real honesty. Real honesty is pure experience. And pure experience is forever ontological.

# 25

# An Interview with Raja Rao

## An interview by Shiva Niranjan

Shiva Niranjan: **Why do you write novels? What do you want to tell your readers through your novels?**

Raja Rao: I do not want to tell them anything. I am a receiver, not a giver. I don't care what people expect, I just enjoy writing. I have often said that for me writing is a *sadhana*, a mode of prayer. Writing is a prayer for me. It gives me pleasure, and I want it to give others pleasure. I write because I wish to write, it's that simple.

**You say writing is a sadhana for you. What do you mean by that?**

Sadhana is what one does as a disciplined practice to reach the spiritual goal. I have endeavoured all my life to be face to face with the Ultimate.

**What is your aesthetic of the novel? How far a departure is it from Western conceptions?**

My aesthetic is to write in the *puranic* tradition. I like the concept of purana; to me that is the only way to conceive a novel. I don't compare my novels with foreign ones—I don't write like a foreign novelist. I am very much an Indian writer, and the Indian form is the puranic form; it comes naturally to me. It would be a mistake to study my novels from a Western viewpoint.

**There are critics who say you are difficult to read because of your many references to metaphysics, myths, and allegories. What do you have to say to that?**

The purana is difficult to read, yes; it is not for everyone. I don't want to compare myself to Kalidasa, say, but Kalidasa is also difficult. He wrote for very few. The goal of an Indian writer should be to aim for the level of *purnadhikara*, to strive for that level. I have no desire to be a popular writer. In fact, my desire is *not* to be a popular writer.

**Your way of writing is quite different from that of Anand, Narayan, or for that matter any author of Indian novels in English. Is there a reason you don't write about the common people of your country, their problems, their suffering? Isn't that also a kind of sadhana?**

No, and why I don't is very simple. The ultimate aim of man is the spiritual, the metaphysical. The Hindu conception of *purushartha*—the four goals of human life—is comprised of righteousness, *dharma;* wealth*, artha;* desire*, kama;* and liberation, *moksha.* If you follow dharma rightly, artha and kama come together, with moksha being the ultimate answer. I see no need, therefore, to write about the poor man because poverty is his dharma.

### What are the main philosophical aspects of your novels?

There is only one: the world ceases to be full of misery the moment one finds one's Guru. I was wavering. I had many questions. Then I met my Guru, and He answered all my questions of a hundred lives.

### So you have ultimate faith in your Guru?

Not merely faith. I would say *shradha,* because shradha includes love.

### Please tell me something about the Sanskrit and French influences on your novels.

The Sanskrit influence I inherited from my family. I was born in an orthodox Brahmin family. At nineteen, being anti-British and a lover of literature, I went to France, not England. The French are intellectually the most advanced people in Europe. France is very much there in my novels. But as I told you, just as I am Indian, so is Sanskrit a part of me. In fact, if asked which influence is the greater, I would say Sanskrit far more than French. Being a more critical language, its influence is there, but nothing compared to Sanskrit. To be honest, though, there is no comparison.

**Please name the French novelist you love most.**

I love Gide and Malraux, two of the greatest French novelists I've read. How much they have influenced me I don't know, but I love them.

**Now, if you please, a word about your development as a novelist.**

After I wrote *Kanthapura,* I grew dissatisfied with my spiritual life and decided not to write anymore. Then I found my Guru, after which it took me years to settle into myself. Once I did, then came *The Serpent and the Rope*, followed by *The Cat and Shakespeare.* In *Kanthapura* I was Gandhian, in *The Serpent and the Rope* I was seeking. *Kanthapura* is quite different from *The Serpent and the Rope.* Though *The Cat and Shakespeare,* too, is different, in essence it is its conclusion.

*Comrade Kirillov* is an earlier novel. Originally written in English, it was first published in French by sheer accident. It shows that a communist can be sincere, but his sincerity is confused, as in intellectual confusion. I actually met a man in England like my character, Kirillov.

**You wrote *Kanthapura* in the 1930s and *The Serpent and the Rope* in the '60s. What prevented you from writing during those three decades?**

As I said, after *Kanthapura* I felt dissatisfied. I was not clear about myself. My prayer was not clear. I did not know what to write, so I vowed not to until I received the ultimate answer I was seeking. Which I did when I found my Guru. Then my wavering was over; hence, *The Serpent and the Rope.*

**I'm curious. In *Kanthapura*, you used names like Waterfall Venkama and Corner House Moorthy, which are rather uncommon in northern India. Such usage is rare in both Hindi and Indian novels in English.**

It is a Mysore tradition; rather, I should say, a Kannada one. For instance, my grand-uncle was living in Hyderabad, where you say *that* house, not my grand-uncle's house. You say that house with the platform in front. It is purely a South-Indian tradition.

**You said that while writing *Kanthapura* you were a Gandhian, but toward the end of the novel we find Moorthy at odds with Gandhi.**

Moorthy was a young man who felt dissatisfied after suffering a defeat, his faith in Gandhi shaken. But the novel projects the Mahatma as his chief inspiration. At one time, Nehru was also dissatisfied with Gandhi's way of struggle. But if Nehru had not been a true Gandhian, India would not be the state we know today. At best, you can say that Moorthy was a *deviating* Gandhian. Nehru, too.

**But a staunch Gandhian like Moorthy ought not to have been frustrated by defeat.**

Cannot a lover of Gandhi be frustrated? Nehru was, and in this way he and Moorthy are alike.

**Assuming *The Serpent and the Rope* a novel of quest, what is the goal of this quest?**

To find an answer to the misery of man, everything from the physical to the intellectual to the spiritual. The hero has everything he humanly needs, yet he is miserable. So the ultimate answer is not human happiness, but ultimate action.

**Do you think the separation between Ramaswamy and Madeleine in *The Serpent and the Rope* was more spiritual than physical in origin?**

Philosophical differences are important; it was on account of these that they finally decided to separate.

**Excuse me, but couldn't you have been a bit more generous to Madeleine?**

In what way?

**I felt she could have lived happily with Ramaswamy.**

But the point is that in trying to become a Buddhist, she was unfair to her own dharma, which was Catholicism. If she had remained a good Catholic, she might have been all right with Ramaswamy.

**So she abandons her dharma and embraces Buddhism, which is quite the opposite of what Ramaswamy believed in, the Advaita Vedanta of Shankara. Are you saying this was the cause of the separation?**

No, not that. Catholicism, again, is much different from Shankara's non-dualism. I am interested in authenticity; one must be authentic, no matter what one professes. For example, having spent quite some time with Gandhi at Sevagram, I have seen him and Maulana Azad talking face to face. Though Gandhi was a good Hindu and Azad a good Muslim, they would speak with authenticity, for they had respect for each other. It is to those who are not authentic that misery comes.

**What inspired you to inject Shankara's non-dualism into *The Serpent and the Rope*?**

I didn't want to inject anything; it just came to me. I was born as I was born. My father did not say, 'I want to project myself in my child.' It just happened, part of the process of creation.

**In *The Serpent and the Rope*, there are discursive passages on myths and metaphysics. Are these deviations from the main plot?**

No, not deviations, but interpretations. They seem to be deviating from the plot only to the superficial reader. In fact, they never do.

**At one place Ramaswamy says, 'I hate this moral India. True Indian morality is based on an ultimate metaphysics.' Is it possible to hate morality and love metaphysics?**

Ramaswamy is not immoral. He is amoral. Is Sri Krishna immoral or amoral in asking Arjuna to go and kill? Sri Krishna is the greatest figure in the world of thinking and literature and is both amoral and metaphysical when he asks Arjuna to kill. Morality is based on necessity. The Vedanta does not talk of morality.

**What is the implication behind the comment in *The Serpent and the Rope*, 'All brides are Benares born?'**

All brides are like Parvathi, though Parvathi was the daughter of the Himalayas. Today, we place her in Kashi, *Annapurne Sadapurna Sankare Pranballabhe*. Every woman is a Parvathi, or potentially so. In the South, and probably the North, a new bride is 'shown the star' in order to be a faithful wife.

**Ramaswamy seems to be a personification of yourself. Is *The Serpent and the Rope* an autobiographical novel?**

Many authors write autobiographically. Ramaswamy is myself, as are Rama Moorthy and Ramakrishna Pai in my other books—or rather, each is an *aspect* of myself. I don't think you can say 'this is me, this is not me.'

**What is the justification for using the name Shakespeare in the title *The Cat and Shakespeare*?**

Because Shakespeare was a sage.

**Is the author of *The Serpent and the Rope* a sage?**

The sage is Truth. The word sage can be defined as a *rishi*, or a guru, or *the* Guru. *The* Guru is the sage of sages. I have sat at the holy feet of a very great sage—my Guru. The disciple of the Guru is a *sadhaka*. My Guru had the compassion to show me the Truth, its naked beauty. Not that I am there yet by any means; I am still trying to be what my Guru taught me to be. The best thing would be to call me a sadhaka. A very serious sadhaka, of course.

**What is the difference between sainthood and sagehood?**

Good question. It is wise to distinguish between a sage and a saint, for sainthood is quite a different thing. The saint is trying to reach God; sainthood is to seek God while striving to be a good man. But the sage is beyond sainthood, above it. Again, the sage is one who is Truth. Sri Krishna was a sage of sages—Sri Rama, too, and Dakshinamoorthy. To me, Shankara was a sage like Krishna, a sage of sages.

When I think of my Guru, if He is all the sands of the oceans taken together, I am not even one grain. I say this with utter sincerity.

**Is there an English parallel to sadhaka?**

One who tries to live what one has been shown to be true is a sadhaka. It is very difficult to find a parallel for it in English. I, for instance, am like the Upanishadic figures Gargi, Nachiketa, and others. I am still trying to live what I have found. The Guru, by contrast, is one who lives it, who is the Truth, already and completely.

## Can the novelist be a sage?

Valmiki was author and sage. In the Sanskrit tradition, the words kavi and rishi are almost the same. The rishi is one who *sees,* who reads what is already there, *drishti.* While the kavi is one who creates. In the Indian tradition the Vedas were written by sages, who were all rishis. The writer and the sage are no different; rishi is the seer, the sage wisdom. Then again, rishi might mean the sage, the seer, *and* the kavi.

My sadhana is to reach that state where this could be true. I am striving to move in that direction. Not that I am there yet, but I continue to struggle.

# Notes

The following notes have been compiled to give the reader, when possible, a look into why these essays, stories, and speeches were written and whether they were published or presented as speeches. Though an incomplete list, and possibly a faulty one in some instances, I have done my best to provide historical information without the author, his friends, and colleagues to consult. A number of journals, books, and organizations that might have helped were also unavailable.

## *Preface*

1. This was taken from the last three paragraphs of a speech Raja Rao presented as a guest lecturer for the conference 'Quest for the Word'. It was held at the State College at Fulton, Johnstown, New York, 13 December 1967.

## The World Is Sound

1. This story was found among the papers of Raja Rao's unpublished novel *The Ganges and Her Sisters*. It, however, was not included in the novel's final manuscript.

## Part I

1. *The Premiere of Sakuntala.* This short story was published in the journal *Asia and the Americas*, June 1943.
2. *A Nest of Singing Birds.* This essay was published in *The Illustrated Weekly of India*, 10 December 1961.
3. *The Poet.* History unknown.
4. *Trois Écrivains Universels.* History unknown.
5. *Gunter Grass: Cat and Mouse.* History unknown.
6. *Thumboo's Krishna.* This was an essay written for an unspecified felicitation in Singapore celebrating Raja's dear friend Dr Edwin Thumboo on 17 December 1991.

    Thumboo's poem 'Krishna' was published in *Westerly*, Vol. 27, No. 2, June 1982.

    Raja Rao's poem 'For Brother Thumboo' was written in conjunction with the essay.
7. *Braj Kachru.* This essay was written for either a publication or event honoring the famous linguist and another of Raja's close friends, Braj Kachru.
8. *Tagore: Renaissance Man.* This was a contribution, in French, to the book *Hommage de la France a Rabindranath Tagore*, published during the Tagore centenary celebrations in France, 1961. It was translated from the French into English by Dr. Mireille T. Chapelle.
9. *Books Which Have Influenced Me.* This piece appeared in *The Illustrated Weekly of India* on 10 February 1963. It

was published again in *Aspects of Indian Writing in English* (edited by M.K. Naik) in 1979.

## Part II

10. *A Fable Goes Round.* History unknown.
11. *The Climate of Indian Literature Today.* This was a work requested by the *New York Times Book Review,* though never appearing there. It was published, however, in *The Literary Criterion*, Vol. X, Winter, 1972. It was republished in *The Literary Criterion: The Raja Rao Centenary Edition* in 2013.
12. *The Story Round, Around Kanthapura.* History unknown.
13. *Why Do You Write?* This essay was written for *Libération,* 1986, a daily newspaper founded in Paris by Jean-Paul Sartre and Serge July.
14. *Two Proposals.* The first, 'In Search of Reality: Cosmology, Poetry, and Linguistics', was an idea for a proposed conference. The second, 'Indian Literature in Search of Form', was part of a paper to be delivered at a meeting of the Modern Language Association of America in New York City. Any further history of both proposals is unknown.
15. An *Irish Interlude.* This essay was published in *The Irish Digest*, September 1966.
16. *The Word.* History unknown.
17. *The English Language and Us.* This speech was given at a British Studies faculty seminar titled 'The Quest for Form: Commonwealth Perspectives' in the Harry Ransom Center at The University of Texas, Austin on 12 February 1982.

18. *Dissolution is Fulfillment.* History unknown.
19. *The West Discovers Sanskrit.* This speech was presented at the international conference 'Toward New Beginnings' hosted by the Indira Gandhi Memorial Trust, New Delhi, in 1987.
20. *The Cave and the Conch: Notes on the Indian Conception of the Word.* This appeared in the book *Indian Writing in English* (edited by Maggie Butcher) in 1983. It contains papers presented by writers and critics at a seminar held at the Commonwealth Institute in London during the International Festival of India in 1982.

## Part III

21. *I Write for Myself.* This interview was published in the Sahitya Akademi's bi-monthly journal *Indian Literature*, No. 126, July–August 1968.
22. *A Conversation with Raja Rao on The Cat and Shakespeare.* This was an interview conducted for *Chandrabhaga: a Magazine of World Writing* in 1979.
23. *Indian English is Sensuous and Silent.* This interview was printed in the newspaper *New Delhi*, 18–31 August 1980.
24. *An Interview with Feroza Jussawalla and Reed Dasenbrock.* This was published in the book *Interviews with Writers of the Post-Colonial World.* These sessions were conducted and edited by Jussawalla and Dasenbrock in 1992.
25. *An interview with Raja Rao.* This appeared in *Indian Writing in English* (edited by Krishna Nandan Sinha) in 1979.

# Acknowledgements

Writing the acknowledgements for this book has been a moving experience.

Though I am thankful for each person and his or her generous contributions, reviewing them collectively has been humbling. Though I have long known the mission of preserving, preparing, and disseminating Raja Rao's life's work was my dharma, I did not have the education or background to carry this out on my own. I am fully aware it was the Guru's Grace alone that provided me the gifted people who flowed into my life to help with the project.

**Richard and Nancy Vaught**, my beloved brother and sister-in-law—out of their love and admiration for Raja Rao, their love for me, and knowing that what I am trying to achieve is a world treasure—have stood by me in every possible way. My thanks to them here is as nothing to what I hold for them in my heart.

My beloved cousin, **Carolyn Gibson**, also has been a source of support and encouragement since the project's inception. Through the many years I was working alone with little to no help, she had perfect faith in my dreams, and remains a champion to me today.

**Patrick Monaghan**, a former student of Raja's, provided not only an extraordinarily magnanimous financial contribution but a brand-new computer array along with an entire office of equipment. His monetary donation alone met the financial needs of the project for many years. Far more than that, his steadfast friendship and support have been a blessing in my life.

After reading Raja Rao's *The Chessmaster and His Moves*, the young **Raman Srinivasan** was so impressed he wanted to meet its author. From the very beginning, a friendship developed destined to become one of the greatest in both men's lives. Though Raja was his mentor, Srinivasan was our guardian, watching over us through the years like a caring son. In addition, few more deeply understand Raja and his writing than he. I will be forever grateful he was part of our lives and remains a part of mine.

Raja was introduced to **Makarand Paranjape** after discovering his brilliant defense of *The Chessmaster and His Moves* in an essay answering critics who did not understand the novel. Makarand and he became friends, and devoted much of his career to making Raja and his works known to the world. Among many other things, he published an anthology, *The Best of Raja Rao,* and wrote a definitive introduction used in Raja's *The Meaning of India* and *Mahatma Gandhi: The Great Indian Way*. I will ever be thankful for Makarand's invaluable contributions to the Raja Rao legacy.

I'd also like to give special thanks to Penguin's **Manasi Subramaniam**, who has helped encourage and guide me on the journey of creating this collection. Included in my thanks is everyone at Penguin Random House India for their excellent support.

The highly respected Austin attorney, **Michael Burk**—and a former student—remained devoted to Raja over the years. As Raja grew elderly, Michael advised that we avail ourselves of legal protections, even providing them as a gift. The papers he drew up repeatedly proved crucial to my husband's safety and well-being throughout a long illness. In addition, he went to great lengths over the years to safeguard Raja's archive and publishing rights. Michael was a tremendous comfort and guide to me when, alone, I found myself having to face what to me at the time was a bewildering multitude of unknowns. I will never forget all that he did for us.

**Angelia McFarland** kindly gave of her brilliant mind and professionally honed organizational skills to create the framework for the Raja Rao Literary Project. First and foremost, it was she who crafted The Sacred Wordsmith nonprofit organization. She also created a highly detailed proposal and financial plan, helped write a national-level grant, and formulated material useful in conferences. She stood by me from the beginning; in fact, so integral is Angelia to the project that I insisted she be by my side at the official signing of Raja's archive over to the Harry Ransom Center in Austin, Texas. I can foresee our personal and working relationship ever growing over time.

Given her career as a gifted teacher and linguaphile, I was both honored and moved when **Dr Mireille Chapelle** offered her skills in translating Raja's essay 'Tagore, Renascence Man' from French into English. The depth of her linguistic sensitivity, her oneness with multiple languages, and wholehearted devotion to the art of translation left me in awe. As I watched her at work, it continually amazed me to see her words transformed as if into music itself. I will always be indebted to Mireille and her remarkable fluency in French for saving so magnificent an essay. As for the deep bond that developed between us while working together, I know it will be lifelong.

I wish to thank **Shri Sudarshan** of the Sanskrit Promotion Foundation for his help in the translation of the book's Sanskrit excerpts. His generous assistance not only made the verses more enjoyable for Sanskrit readers but gave the entire book an aura of ancient beauty.

Now, to my editor. The prize-winning novelist **J. Michael Dolan**, through writing his own books and after decades of study, had learned the intricacies of both copy and developmental editing. I never cease to wonder at his mastery of syntax, grammar, punctuation, and style. Even more wondrous was how he ended up joining me in the project. Though I'd had a long association with his family, I'd never met Michael—until the day he appeared unexpectedly at my door.

His ability to polish rough drafts to a fine sheen, while carefully adhering to Raja's intent, proved invaluable. Indeed, this book would never have happened without him, its glorious essays forever lost to history. For all this, and our friendship, there are no words large enough to express my thanks.

Susan Raja-Rao, Austin, Texas
Thanksgiving Day, 2021